A FORCE FOR NATURE

THE ENVIRONMENTAL LITIGATION

OF

LEWIS C. GREEN

BY

FLORENCE SHINKLE

AND

PATRICIA TUMMONS

GASHOUSE
BOOKS

Gashouse Books
PO Box 5131
St. Louis, MO 63139

Library of Congress Control Number: 2009942146

ISBN: 978-0-9800475-6-1

Cover photograph from the *St. Louis Globe-Democrat* Archives of the St. Louis Mercantile Library at the University of Missouri–St. Louis.

Printed in the United States of America
15 16 17 18 19   5 4 3 2

CONTENTS

Foreword

*"The ultimate measure of a man is not where he stands in moments of comfort and
convenience, but where he stands at times of challenge and controversy."*
—Martin Luther King (1963)

LEWIS GREEN WAS A FIGHTER. HE WAS A MASTER OF THE HAND-TO-HAND COMBAT
involved in high-stakes legal battles, but also deeply understood the
broader political and economic forces acting upon the generals in the
field. He outmaneuvered many of his adversaries in environmental
lawsuits, creating ripples of change emanating from the courtroom into
society at large. As an environmentalist, I am thankful that this talented
man chose as his mission the cause of saving our imperiled planet.

Authors Patricia Tummons and Florence Shinkle have painted a
colorful portrait of the body of work of one of the country's earliest
and greatest environmental litigators. It is a story about a smart and
dedicated lawyer who looked after the laws passed in the heyday of
the environmental movement. This book will be of special interest to
Missourians who work to protect the air, water, and land. But it is also a
larger story about one of the pioneers of using the courts to ensure that
environmental laws passed with great fanfare were not later forgotten.

What Lew Green realized was that the legislative victories of the late
1960s and early 1970s would not automatically translate into a cleaner
environment. Instead, the passage of a significant new law means years
of rulemakings and seemingly endless battles to have it enforced. These
later steps in the process—largely hidden from the light of day—are often where real progress is won or lost. While the work is tremendously
important, it takes a steely will and steady devotion to weather the often
hostile winds that buffet environmental advocates along the way.

Lew had the temperament and intellectual capacity to effectively en-
gage in this process. When he took on a case he had no illusions about the
potholes and curves in the road ahead. He knew that judges sometimes
place a very skeptical eye on environmentalists who take their grievances

to court. He knew it was going to be a slog, and that one had to be in it for the long haul or it wasn't even worth beginning. Lawyers for opposing parties knew this about him too, which undoubtedly made him more successful. They knew that if the case was important enough for Lew to get involved, then they were going to have to fight it to the bitter end as well.

Lew and his clients usually came away with something for which the public can now be thankful. The air in Missouri is considerably cleaner as a result of years of up-and-down litigation that forced regulators, industry, and the public to come to grips with needed changes. There are more numerous, more natural parks around St. Louis because of his efforts to keep greenspace in public ownership. There is a football stadium in downtown St. Louis today as opposed to its being in the floodplain of the Missouri River. And citizen groups have at least a partially opened door to the courthouse as a result of repeated efforts to demonstrate the legitimacy of environmental injuries.

Only a few of these results came from clear-cut legal victories where one could stand on the courthouse steps and crow. Instead, as most litigators can attest, a lawsuit is an arduous, tedious, and costly process that often takes many years to go from start to finish. In part because litigation is this way, no one—be they government agencies, businesses, or individuals—relishes the thought of being sued or even having to sue someone else. This process can take a toll on anyone, particularly under-funded and over-stretched public interest litigators.

Lew Green knew that the mere ability and willingness of an environmental group to take someone to court has a deterrent effect beyond the scope of any particular case. The impact of his long career was felt as much through the cases he didn't have to bring as those that he did. This is because regulatory agencies were aware that if they overstepped their bounds for reasons of political expediency they would have to explain themselves to a judge. And businesses that pushed beyond the limits of the law knew that they faced a real risk of becoming entangled in costly litigation.

The story of air pollution control in the St. Louis region is perhaps Lew's greatest achievement and is illustrative of his many battles. After nearly two decades of slower than desired progress on air pollution throughout the country, in 1990 Congress decided to put clear deadlines into the federal Clean Air Act. These deadlines meant that regions with dirty air—such as St. Louis—had to get their act together and bring pollution levels down to a certain level by a certain date.

Predictably, there was a lot of hand-wringing in Missouri about the threatened economic consequences of reducing pollution. The low-hanging fruit had already been plucked in the early days of air pollution control, but it turned out to not be enough to meet federal standards. Now came the hard part of bringing about changes that affected large numbers of people, such as limiting the tailpipe emissions from cars. The Missouri General Assembly, Missouri Department of Natural Resources, and U.S. EPA predictably dawdled in the face of a possible political backlash.

Had the Sierra Club and Coalition for the Environment not had Lew Green on their side to hold these entities' feet to the fire, it could be that the Clean Air Act would have forever sat gathering dust on the shelf. However, years of back-and-forth litigation with the EPA prompted action and, eventually, cleaner air. What is illustrative about the case is that there was no crowning moment when a judge ordered the air to be cleaner. Instead, it was a years-long battle, involving some wins, some losses, and ultimately ending with a whimper when the desired result of cleaner air made the case moot.

Lew was the legal mastermind that converted environmental ideals into tangible action, but one should not overlook his equally capable and dedicated supporting cast. There are Leo and Kay Drey, ardent conservationists from St. Louis who also had the capacity to fund some of the expensive litigation endeavors. There was Roger Pryor, the widely known leader of the Coalition for the Environment, a frequent plaintiff in suits brought by Lew Green. And there is Lew's wife, Louise, who kindly supported him through many years of long hours and minimal compensation for his work.

In addition, Lew found a number of other lawyers who, like him, were willing to sacrifice their time and personal finances to represent the public interest in court. His firm did have paying clients, but the income from this work was often used to subsidize the environmental cases that seemed to be the attorneys' collective passion. One former colleague notes that even Lew apparently had his limits, recounting an occasional threat that if the firm lost money three years in a row he would "close it up." Of course, this is not a financial benchmark shared by many other law firm managing partners.

I remember the day in 2003 that I learned that Lew had passed away. I was driving down a long, lonely road in Missouri's bootheel checking up on a proposed Corps of Engineers' drainage project that environmentalists were fiercely opposing. At the time, I worked for the Coalition for the Environment and was trying to emulate his inspiring work, along with that of Roger Pryor and the Dreys, all people I had read about in the paper when I was growing up.

Even though Lew was many years my senior, and I had only known him for a few years, his death hit me hard. In part, this was because the environmental movement about which I cared a lot had just lost one of its titans, but in larger measure because Lew had become a good friend and valued mentor. What I admired most is that he could be a ferocious advocate and firm believer in the cause, but he also did not take himself so seriously that he could not also have a good time while doing his work.

Many found Lew to be intimidating and tough as nails. He had a humbling pedigree, including graduating with high honors from Harvard Law School (in an era when such honors were very stingily given out) and clerking for a U.S. Supreme Court justice. He had a razor sharp mind, a quick, biting wit, and stared out from behind large, hawkish glasses. He had a reputation for not suffering fools. But beneath it all he was in reality an extremely funny, playful, and good-natured man. Even in the midst of gut-wrenching and tiring litigation in which he and others had invested their hearts and souls, he could let go a zinger that would lighten the mood and put things in perspective.

One of my first encounters with him was in the early days of my time at the Coalition for the Environment. I had walked in half-way through the long battle with the federal EPA over air pollution regulations. While I was still very much a rookie and did not know much of anything about the case, Lew suggested we write an op-ed piece for the *St. Louis Post-Dispatch*. After sending him a rather mundane draft to review, I got back an edited version with a little more flair. "Gotta give the editors some red meat," he said, knowing that the editorial board would feel compelled to pare back our advocate's perspective. This was the kind of good humor that brought joy to our difficult and sometimes demoralizing task.

Lew's legal work lives on today in the form of the Great Rivers Environmental Law Center, a non-profit law firm he founded shortly before his death. His daughter Kathleen Henry, his long-time law partner Bruce Morrison, and skillful advocate Henry Robertson continue to litigate the type of cases that Lew pursued for so many years. For the sake of our environment, let's hope that this serves as a lasting legacy to one of our nation's environmental pioneers.

Introduction

In the Political Trenches: Green's Early Environmental Work

Eliot F. Porter

Porter was the Executive Secretary of the Air Conservation Commission from 1966 to 1969.

When, or how, Lewis Green first developed an interest in air pollution is not entirely clear. It may have had some relationship to the fact that he suffered somewhat from asthma and hay fever, though perhaps a stronger connection was to his love of nature and the natural environment, coupled with a modestly ambitious interest in politics.

Those interests began to become realized during the Democratic primary campaign for governor of Missouri in 1964. Green was at the time committeeman of the Bonhomme Township Democratic Club, the members of which included many friends who shared his concern about the environment. The club campaigned hard, and successfully, for the nomination of Warren E. Hearnes of Charleston, in the southeast corner of the state. At the time, Hearnes was majority leader in the Missouri House of Representatives.

Hearnes's wife, Betty, recalled the campaign vividly. She remembered accompanying her husband to 14 coffees, at which he gave 14 speeches in a single day in St. Louis County. Often they had been arranged by Green, who also wrote, or helped write, many of the speeches.

The support of the Bonhomme Township Democrats and their political companions was a great help to Hearnes. He won handily both in the primary and the general election in St. Louis City and County. Betty Hearnes said that her husband and Green "didn't always agree, but they were friends and stayed friends, and that doesn't always happen in politics."

It was at those gatherings in St. Louis County that talk turned to the poor quality of air in the St. Louis area and what could be done about it.

1

Hearnes was accustomed to the clean country air in Missouri's Bootheel, where he lived. He could not help but notice the leaden skies of St. Louis. He made cleaning up the air one of his campaign pledges and enlisted Green to write some of his speeches.

After his election, Hearnes supported enactment of Missouri's first air pollution control law, and in October of 1965, Hearnes named Green chairman of the Air Conservation Commission that the legislation created. The agency's curious, and not entirely logical, name—unique in the United States—may reflect an effort by the legislation's sponsor, Senator Maurice Schechter of Creve Coeur, to avoid the word control, which conservative members of the Legislature might have found off-putting.

Green's appointment was one of those cases, uncommon in the annals of American politics, where a reward to a supporter did not involve any financial benefit, nor even much prospect of one. Commission members served without pay and, in Green's case, at some cost. He later estimated that his work as commission chairman consumed half his time. His law practice must have suffered.

Only once during Green's tenure as chairman did Hearnes intervene in the commission's mission, and he did it delicately. Among the first regulations the commission promulgated for the St. Louis area was a ban on leaf burning. There was, of course, a public outcry. Burning fallen leaves was an autumnal ritual, especially in the well-shaded suburbs of St. Louis County. The smell of burning leaves was pleasant and a seasonal phenomenon many people looked forward to, much as children look forward to the first snowfall—and they were not going to forego it lightly.

The problem created by leaf burning was that it occurred at the very time of year that the pollutants were most likely to be trapped under a dome of warm air, a phenomenon known as atmospheric inversion.

It happened that at the very time the leaf burning ban was proposed Hearnes was being challenged for re-election by Lawrence K. Roos, the Republican chief executive of St. Louis County. Roos and his supporters characterized the leaf burning ban as regulatory overkill and the kind of bureaucratic interference with an agreeable and harmless custom that was typical of Democrats.

Rather than try to debate the issue on its merits, Hearnes quietly, politely, and somewhat obliquely advised Green that it would be awkward for his re-election effort were the leaf burning rule to take effect during the campaign. Thus, at Green's instigation, the commission agreed to postpone the effective date of the ban for a year.

Hearnes was delighted. He held a press conference in St. Louis to announce the postponement, which was well-publicized. Only the editorial page of the *St. Louis Post-Dispatch* struck a discordant note, pointing out that the delay clearly had been arranged for Hearnes's political convenience.

A touch of history: In the late 1930s the air in St. Louis passed up that of Pittsburgh as the smuttiest in the nation. In fact, it rivaled that of London, the Ruhr, and the industrial Midlands of England.

The main culprit was coal smoke, which, when combined with St. Louis's frequent periods of atmospheric stagnation, sometimes required that streetlights remain on all day. St. Louis was nourished on coal in those days. High-sulfur soft coal mostly from the pits of southern Illinois just a few miles away across the Mississippi heated its homes, schools, offices, and public buildings, generated its electricity, and fueled its factories. Most of the buildings of downtown St. Louis were heated by low-pressure steam piped from an elderly coal-fired electric power plant on the riverfront. Look in the cellar of any St. Louis dwelling more than 70 years old, and many much younger, and you can find the ghostly vestiges of a coal bin and in the alley out back the remnants of the concrete sarcophagi into which householders dumped their ashes.

In desperation, the city retained Raymond Tucker, an engineer, to act as its smoke control czar. Tucker and his small army of inspectors attacked the problem mainly by requiring coal-burning installations either to convert to oil or natural gas or to operate more efficiently so that the particles of carbon flying up the stack would be consumed in the boiler instead.

The Tucker reformation was immensely successful—as far as it went. Tucker was made a hero and went on to become mayor of St. Louis, and later an arterial street was renamed in his honor. But his achievement did not address such insidious and largely invisible pollutants such as oxides of sulfur (the products of burning sulfur-bearing coal) nor the complex and likewise invisible airborne broth from automobile exhaust, which, in the presence of sunlight, becomes the photochemical smog, so prevalent in Southern California.

By the time Hearnes took office, the term air pollution had become part of the language. There had been a number of dramatic episodes such as one in Donora, Pennsylvania, (Stan Musial's hometown) in 1948, which took the lives of 22 people, and one in London in 1962, where the death toll ran into the hundreds. Both of these episodes were characterized by a combination of phenomena in which the uncontrolled emission of pollutants became trapped under a ceiling of stagnant air. While these events engaged the public's attention, they also reinforced the politically conservative view that air pollution was a purely local situation—a neighborhood nuisance writ large—that ought properly to be dealt with by local governments.

But at the time the air pollution law was introduced into the Missouri Legislature, this view was pretty much on the defensive. Besides Governor Hearnes's backing, the legislation had the active support of the liberal Democratic delegations from the St. Louis and Kansas City areas, led by Maurice Schechter.

Probably the greatest impetus to the passage of Missouri's clean air law was the spectre of federal intervention, a prospect horrifying to many Missouri politicians, should the states fail to act. The federal air pollution control administration was in the final year of an exhaustive three-year study of the air quality in the two-state St. Louis metropolitan area. Scores of air sampling instruments were placed throughout the region to gather data by the hour, day, and year.

While the project included token participation by state and local governments and even by industry representatives, it was predominantly a federal project. Federal personnel designed the study, selected the sites for the sampling instruments, governed the statistical analysis of the data, wrote the final five-volume report, and paid most of the bills. The study concluded with an array of recommendations, which provided the template for the regulations adopted by Missouri and independently by St. Louis and St. Louis County—but not by Illinois, nor any of the local governments on the Illinois side of the St. Louis region.

The approach used in the regulations was to start with ambient air quality standards (actually goals) for various pollutants, setting forth the degree of pollution deemed tolerable, and to work back from there to specific emission rules for various sources calculated to achieve those

standards. This process, which the feds termed "air quality management," always made Green uncomfortable since it would allow pollution
sources to continue their emissions so long as the air quality standards
were met. It was tantamount, he often said privately, to issuing licenses
to pollute.

Publicly, however, Green bit his tongue, probably in deference to
the fact that the federal government was subsidizing Missouri with both
technical expertise and substantial start-up funds. Later, after Green retired from the commission, he openly ridiculed the process.

The argument was at that time largely theoretical, however. The
state's metropolitan areas were nowhere near meeting the air quality
standards recommended by the three-year study. For example, the standard adopted for airborne particulate matter (a catchall term for soot,
dust, fly ash, and the like) in the St. Louis region was 75 micrograms per
cubic meter of air on an annual geometric average. (A microgram is a
millionth of a gram; 75 micrograms is about the weight of a fly's wing. A
geometric average—the nth root of n pieces of data multiplied together—
tends to dampen high measurements.) The standard for sulfur dioxide
was a concentration of one tenth of a part per million parts of air. (That's
roughly equivalent to a jigger of vermouth in ten tank cars of gin.)

The Air Conservation Commission's tiny staff was initially housed in
Jefferson City in an ornate Second Empire building with 15-foot ceilings
and marble fireplaces that once housed the federal court and post office.
Since it was viewed generally as out of date (bureaucrats are not known
for their reverence for antiquity), it had been turned over to the state
government's stepchildren. Other occupants included the state water
pollution control agency.

It is doubtful that there has ever been before or since a more acces-
sible or transparent state agency in Missouri. Nor a more informal one.
One of the staffers kept his yellow parakeet (named Pease Blossom) at
the office, where it flew about purloining small objects such as pencils
and paper clips, while leaving small deposits of guano on the furniture.
Newspaper reporters and environmental activists mainly from St. Louis
and Kansas City came and went freely, helping themselves to the office
coffee and rummaging through the files, sometimes without troubling
to ask permission.

Air pollution was front-page news in those days, and the Jefferson City bureaus of the *Post-Dispatch* and *Globe-Democrat* of St. Louis and the *Kansas City Star* competed vigorously for scoops. The monthly meetings of the commission were thoroughly covered. When the Air Conservation Commission adopted comprehensive clean air regulations for the St. Louis area, it was a front-page story.

All of which was in accordance with Green's unstated but clearly apparent doctrine that the way to achieve a social purpose such as clean air was to keep the public well-informed and friendly. His pick for the agency's first executive secretary—that is, its chief of staff—was a newspaper reporter with no experience in chemistry or engineering, much less the rather recondite subspecialty of air pollution control.

Industry representatives who complained that air pollution rulemaking involved lawyers practicing science and scientists practicing law never mentioned journalists, who were doubtless beneath their contempt.

Notwithstanding the happy and collegial atmosphere in the office, the commission and its staff faced a sea of troubles. After a brownout in St. Louis during the steaming summer of 1966, owing to the failure of Union Electric to keep up with the demand for air conditioning, the Missouri Public Service Commission proposed a change in the law to give it veto power over air pollution regulations relating to electric utilities. It was a proactive move, since clean air regulations had not yet taken effect and thus had no relevance to Union Electric's difficulties.

Green's response was to insist that the PSC's proposal be considered jointly by the two commissions. Several hearings were held with the chairmen of the two commissions presiding side by side, while engineers from the state's power companies tried to prove that air pollution control would cripple them and plunge the state into sweltering darkness. The atmosphere was as tense and hostile as a murder trial.

The matter came to a close, when Green, objecting to a procedural point, walked out. The PSC let its proposal drop.

Later, Peabody Coal Co., based in St. Louis, brought a lawsuit against the Air Conservation Commission to block the regulation limiting the sulfur content of coal. The commission, represented by then-state Attorney General John C. Danforth, fought back vigorously. The turning point in the case was the testimony of a pulmonary specialist describing in plain but vivid language how sulfur dioxide deadens the cilia in the trachea, impairing their ability to capture and expel inhaled particles. The judge, victim himself of a chronic respiratory disorder, listened intently and at the next recess invited the witness into his chambers. Shortly afterward, Peabody not only withdrew its lawsuit, but opened a new mine in Illinois to supply the low-sulfur coal it had previously claimed did not exist nearby.

Prominent, though unsuccessful, among Green's efforts as chairman of the Air Conservation Commission was his attempt to create interstate agreements, one between Missouri and Kansas for joint control of air pollution in the Kansas City area, and another between Missouri and Illinois, for the St. Louis area. Both regions straddle state lines, both have sources of air pollution on both sides of the border, and in both regions contaminants drift back and forth, making it often impossible to pinpoint which of many sources is the origin of each lungful of polluted air.

Green argued, and many agreed, that a regional agency, established by compact between the states, would, by imposing uniform regulations throughout a metropolitan area, insure fairness and prevent one state from luring industry from its neighbor with promises of more lenient rules. And while it would not be absolutely immune from political pressure—for nothing ever is—an interstate agency would at least be partly insulated from purely local influence of cities and counties in its region of jurisdiction.

Green had some powerful voices in his corner, including Governor Hearnes and former St. Louis Mayor Tucker. Tucker said that without an interstate agency to impose uniform rules, he doubted that control of air pollution in the St. Louis area would ever be possible.

Green made himself an expert on the law and history of interstate compacts. He theorized, and often said, in an appeal to politicians jealous of states' rights, that a compact agency with vigorous enforcement powers would forestall direct intervention by the federal government to clean up the air in the Kansas City and St. Louis regions. He and members of the Air Conservation Commission staff arranged several meetings between Hearnes and the governors of Illinois and Kansas. The meetings were friendly and encouraging. The three governors (all Democrats) appeared to agree that putting air pollution in the two metropolitan areas under the control of bi-state authorities was the sensible thing to do. So did many members of the three state legislatures.

But the results were disappointing. The Missouri General Assembly approved a clean air compact (of which Green was principal author) for the Kansas City metropolitan area, but the Kansas Legislature balked. A clean air compact for the St. Louis area never got beyond the talking stage.

Green's chairmanship of the commission came to an abrupt and somewhat inglorious end in the spring of 1969. The commission's budget had become stalled in the state Senate for reasons unclear both to Green and agency staff. The key figure was Senator John Downes of St. Joseph, who, like Green, was a Harvard graduate, a liberal Democrat, and the General Assembly's leading intellect—and leading wit. Green had always considered him an ally.

The commission's executive secretary and his wife, who was active in liberal Democratic politics and on good terms with Downes, paid Downes a visit to find out what the problem might be. Your problem, Downes told them bluntly, was Green. "Get rid of your wicked captain and your ship will right herself. Tell him to resign.

"And none of this Sydney Carton stuff either," he added. "Tell him just quietly to resign."

Downes did not expatiate on his animus toward Green, and his interlocutors were too stunned to ask. It may have had something to do with what Green had said or done as leader of the Bonhomme Township Democratic organization—something Downes perceived as a betrayal. Or it may have been something more sinister, relating to air pollution control. If Green ever found out, he kept it to himself.

When Downes's declaration was passed on to Green, he immediately and without a whimper of complaint tendered his resignation to the governor. The chairmanship passed to James Bogle, owner of a 7,000-acre farm in the Bootheel, a neighbor of Governor Hearnes, and one of the charter members of the commission. Though nominally a Republican, and a political conservative, Bogle had become through his experience on the commission a convert to the cause of clean air.

Several years later, Green said he had few regrets. "They couldn't take much away from me because I was already devoting half my time to the job"— time that would otherwise have been devoted to his private law practice.

In late August 1969, three months after Green's departure from the commission, the St. Louis region experienced an air pollution "episode" of the Donora-London variety. It lasted about five days, caused considerable discomfort and illness and perhaps some fatalities. Most conspicuously, it engendered public outrage and focused attention on air pollution to a degree not seen since the Raymond Tucker era.

Thomas Eagleton, then a member of the Senate subcommittee on air and water pollution, seized the opportunity to hold a day-long hearing in St. Louis. Green was among those testifying.

He did not discuss the August episode directly, but instead called into question the conceptual framework underlying the nation's approach to air pollution—air quality management, in the patois of federal clean air authorities. That approach, borrowed from the field of water pollution control (where it made more sense), was the three-step process of sampling air quality, setting air quality goals, and finally establishing limits on emissions intended to achieve those goals.

The problem with this approach, Green testified, was that it places the burden of proof on local clean air agencies to show what levels of pollution are harmful and, next, to justify emission limits calculated to achieve those goals, if only just barely. Also it allowed—indeed, encouraged—different standards from state to state and even within the same state. Thus, the standard for airborne particles adopted by the Missouri Air Conservation Commission for the Kansas City area was more stringent than that for the St. Louis area. The only justification for this difference was that Kansas City air was cleaner to begin with, so the goals would be easier to attain.

The entire process, Green declared, amounted to an invitation to polluters to challenge both the air quality goals as stricter than necessary to protect health, and the emission limits as more rigorous than necessary to achieve those goals.

"No single aspect of our national air pollution control program is more degrading, destructive or misguided," Green told Eagleton. Congress, he said, should abandon the notion, graven in the federal Clean Air Act, that air pollution is a purely local or regional problem, and recognize that it is a national—indeed, global—one. As proof, he cited the rising concentrations of lead in Arctic ice, the fact that pesticides drift thousands of miles, and the buildup of carbon dioxide that is heating up the entire planet.

Highlights of Green's Tenure
With the Air Conservation Commission

"Accomplishments of the last three years are somewhat more than I expected," Lewis Green said in a 1968 interview with Robert Koebbe of the *St. Louis Globe-Democrat*, "but not beyond what I dreamed."

What Green himself identified as highlights of his tenure as chairman of the Missouri Air Conservation Commission included:

• The out-of-court settlement with Peabody Coal Co., which had challenged air pollution regulations established by the Air Conservation Commission. This, Green told Koebbe, "has to be the most satisfying" of all his achievements.

• The adoption of stringent air-pollution regulations for the St. Louis and Kansas areas.

• The hiring of a staff with the competence to police air quality.

Green identified vehicle emissions as the biggest air pollution problem facing the nation.

As for disappointments, Green lamented his inability to work out an interstate compact with Illinois: "We never found anyone in Illinois who would introduce a compact that was not an industry proposal," Green was quoted as having said.

"Although we lack an interstate agreement, which is really needed to solve the metropolitan problem, we must continue doing the job in Missouri, to show other states it can be done," Green said.

Chapter I

A Golf Course at Queeny
Is Denied After Two Decades
of Litigation

Patricia Tummons

"The Queeny farm was the most beautiful open land," recalls Kay Drey of the 600 or so acres that later became Queeny Park. "It would have been one of the most beautiful ready-made parks in the Midwest. All you had to do was hang out a sign and let the people come in."

In the course of the county's efforts to obtain the tract, Drey says, "The Open Space Council had a meeting at the Queeny land. Wayne Kennedy, parks director for St. Louis County, told us the county wouldn't do any development there," a statement that helped the county earn the support of the council, which Drey's husband, Leo, had helped to found.

But, as with so many other promises of the county under the administration of Lawrence K. Roos, that was a promise observed in the breach. And so, practically from the day St. Louis County acquired the land, Drey has refused to visit the park. It breaks her heart, she says, to see the plethora of buildings and installations—a convention center, swimming pool, and dog museum, among them—that have been developed at the site, detracting from the park's natural features.

Still, it could have been much worse: county officials also were proposing to build a golf course at Queeny Park. Thanks to the efforts of Lewis Green, representing Drey and others who felt a keen sense of betrayal at the prospect, that proposal came to naught, as did the county's

11

plan to fund the developments out of taxpayer revenue, in direct violation of a promise made at the time voters approved acquisition of the park land. In the process, Green also won a ruling that effectively reaffirmed the public's right to know what its elected and appointed officials were doing.

A PURCHASE DEFERRED

IN THE 1950S, EDGAR MONSANTO QUEENY, AN EXECUTIVE WITH THE ST. LOUIS–based Monsanto Co., had offered his estate to St. Louis County for use as a park. The county administration rejected the offer, saying it would be too expensive to maintain. At the time, the county leaders simply could not imagine that future growth would put open space at a premium.

A decade later, St. Louis County released a study, "The Challenge of Growth," that called for the acquisition of thousands of acres of land for future parks. Spurred by the report, in 1966, the newly formed St. Louis Open Space Council conducted a petition drive to place a proposition on the ballot that would have authorized the county to issue up to $25 million in general obligation bonds to acquire some 6,000 acres, including the Queeny tract, for 24 parks.

Once again, the county's acquisition of the Queeny land was put off. The referendum won a large majority of the vote, but fell short of the needed two-thirds majority by a heartbreaking 376 votes out of the total 76,854 cast.

In 1969, County Supervisor Lawrence K. Roos and County Parks Director Wayne Kennedy approached the Open Space Council with a proposal that again sought voter approval for acquisition of park lands. This time, two questions regarding parks would be put to the voters. The first was a proposition asking for approval of a total of $19.38 million in general obligation bonds, of which $15.61 million would be used to purchase 2,800 acres (including the 675-acre Queeny tract) and $3.77 million would be used for improvements at 23 existing parks. The second proposition sought approval of $5.5 million in revenue bonds to be used to develop recreational amenities, including golf courses, at three of the sites to be purchased with G.O. bonds.

The Open Space Council was not enthusiastic about the recreational facilities, but it lent its support to both propositions. In addition, Roos pressed the business organization Civic Progress to get behind the plan. With funds from that group, the public relations firm Fleishman-Hillard was engaged to launch a campaign, run in close collaboration with Roos and Kennedy.

In maps and other materials distributed to the media, community groups, and the general public, the proposed recreational facilities (swimming pools, golf courses, ice rinks) were mapped on three sites totaling 800 acres to be purchased in the north, west central, and south parts of the county. No facilities were proposed for the Queeny tract or any of the other parks to be acquired or enlarged through land purchases. In fact, development of the Queeny tract was to be minimal—a parking lot, restrooms, picnic areas and shelters, perhaps a playground. The more intensive recreational developments, such as the golf courses and recreational centers, were to be self-supporting, paid for with user fees.

In the weeks leading up to the vote, time and again, county officials stressed this point. Kennedy and his staff "spoke at meetings almost every noon and night during the entire time from probably the middle of April until June 3, five days a week," Green would later write. At these engagements, they would pass out a small flier prepared by Fleishman-Hillard, which stated in part: "Get more parks before the land is gone," and "make wholesome recreation available (no cost to taxpayer)."

On June 3, 1969, voters in St. Louis County approved the acquisition of the park land by a vote of 78,407 to 35,816. The proposition calling for revenue bonds for recreational facilities was approved by a slightly higher margin, 79,894 to 34,677.

As early as September 11, 1969, the first of three installments of the general obligation bonds was sold. By March 1971, the entire authorized amount, $19.38 million, had been raised in the bond market.

A TOUGH SELL

SELLING THE REVENUE BONDS WAS NOT SO EASY. BONDING COMPANIES TENDED TO view such instruments as having a high risk. In addition, Missouri law capped at 8 percent the interest rates that municipalities could pay on any bonds, making it all the more unlikely that the revenue bonds for the golf courses and recreational centers would attract any interest from the bond market.

This concern was spelled out by the three bankers sitting on the county's Investment Advisory Board. Barely a year after the propositions were approved, committee members Roland C. Behrens, Wilbur H. Eckstein, and Roy W. Jordan gave Roos the financial equivalent of a cold shower.

The committee had polled a number of bond houses locally and nationally to determine whether the recreational bonds could be marketed. On June 4, 1970, Behrens wrote Roos: "In my opinion, these bonds are unmarketable at this time or in the near future. . . . Bonds which are secured by revenues of public recreational facilities with no other security provided are generally rated of inferior quality and have very limited marketability under the best of circumstances."

Roos had proposed that a "feasibility study" of the planned facilities might give assurances to the bond market. Behrens disagreed, quoting the opinion of one of the bankers surveyed: "Having a feasibility study made would in no way change the general nature of the credit . . . it would be wishful thinking to try to sell these bonds or to try any attempts at promotion to sell them."

"It would seem the county may have to resubmit the issue to the electorate so as to provide payment primarily from user revenues with any deficiency assumed by the county," Behrens concluded.

But going back to the electorate was not what Roos or Kennedy had in mind. In a letter in late 1971, Kennedy acknowledged that "it would be embarrassing" to go back to the public for approval of a different plan to finance the recreational developments. Instead, Roos approached officials of the Monsanto Company, in the hope that in honor of their former executive, the firm would contribute funds for the recreational facilities. As described in the brief to the Appeals Court, "A Monsanto official suggested that [Roos] contact Mrs. Edgar Queeny. . . . It was also suggested that he ask General Leif Sverdrup of [the engineering firm] Sverdrup & Parcel . . . to go with him to talk to Mrs. Queeny." In their discussions with her, Roos and Sverdrup suggested that "a wonderful way to memorialize her husband's name would be to erect something in Queeny Park, and they told her that if she did this the park would be named after her late husband. They talked in broad terms of a family recreational area."

"From the beginning of the discussions with Mrs. Queeny," Green wrote, "Supervisor Roos planned that the recreational facilities which would be placed in Queeny Park, in accordance with the proposal he made to Mrs. Queeny, would be one of the three recreational complexes which the voters had been told would be financed with the proceeds of the revenue bonds approved on June 3, 1969. At no time did Supervisor Roos tell Mrs. Queeny that the campaign literature . . . had stated that the three recreation centers would be placed on 800 acres additional to and apart from the Queeny tract."

After Mrs. Queeny indicated her willingness to make a gift to the county, Roos then contacted Edward Greensfelder (his first cousin) and the Greensfelder Foundations (of which Sverdrup was a trustee). Both Mrs. Queeny and the Greensfelder Foundations eventually made commitments of $1 million each.

With those pledges in hand, Roos asked Sverdrup & Parcel to begin developing a master plan for recreational facilities in Queeny Park. The next step was to develop a prospectus and feasibility study, and for this the county engaged the firm of Lybrand, Ross Bros. & Montgomery. To help market the bonds, the county retained a "triumvirate" of three brokerage houses, G.H. Walker of St. Louis, Stern Brothers of Kansas City, and White, Weld of Chicago, which would receive a fee of half a percent of the par value of the bonds.

The public sale of the $5.5 million in revenue bonds was scheduled to occur on May 4, 1972. But even as the master plan, feasibility study, and prospectus were distributed widely to bond underwriters, the county refused to disclose any of the documents to members of the public who were growing increasingly concerned that the county's rumored plans would breach promises made in the campaign to win approval of the ballot propositions.

SECRET STUDIES

AGAINST THIS BACKGROUND, IN APRIL 1972, THREE CITIZENS—LEO DREY, William Bueler, and Betty Cunningham—retained Lewis Green to represent them in a suit against Roos and Kennedy, seeking to force the county to disclose the prospectus and feasibility study and to block the use of any proceeds from the sale of general obligation bonds for the planning, design, or construction of recreational facilities that voters were told would be paid for by user fees.

The plaintiffs sought a temporary restraining order barring the defendants from proceeding with any plans to build any of the recreational facilities called out in the Queeny feasibility study, "or committing or spending general obligation bond proceeds or general revenue funds to develop a recreational center anywhere."

After a day of arguments on a Saturday in his chambers, Judge George Schaaf allowed Drey and Green to see a copy of the feasibility study, but they could not show it or divulge its contents to anyone else. On April 28, Schaaf signed an order enjoining the county from proceeding with any plans to build a recreational center, although he did not bar the sale of revenue bonds.

But Schaaf also was requiring the plaintiffs to post a bond against damages in the event that the county eventually prevailed in court. According to Kay Drey, Leo and the other defendants did not want to expose themselves to the threat of any counter-claim from the county, and so on April 29, the lawsuit was withdrawn and the restraining order was lifted.

Three days later, on May 2, Green filed a second lawsuit, this time on behalf of Kay Drey, Adele Tuchler, and Marian Bueler. The claims were much the same as in the first lawsuit, but, as Kay explained, the three new plaintiffs were "legally impecunious"—they had no significant assets that would be at risk should the county file a counter-claim for damages. That did not stop the county from trying. Just a week after the complaint was filed, the county lodged a counter-claim, alleging that the plaintiffs knew that their suit would result in either no bids being received for the revenue bonds or if bids were received they would be at a much higher interest rate and at a higher discount. "The purpose, motive, and the intent [of the plaintiffs] was not to enjoin St. Louis County from constructing a golf course on Queeny Park but was to jeopardize the sale of revenue bonds," the county claimed, seeking $250,000 in actual damages and $300,000 in punitive damages.

Green asked the court to decree that revenue bonds "must be self-supporting, and the principal and interest may be paid off only out of the net revenues derived from user fees." The court was also asked to find that the county could not lawfully pledge any operating funds to retire the bonds, could not locate the proposed recreational center in Queeny Park, and, finally, could not continue to withhold from public view the prospectus or feasibility study "or other information relating to the county's use of public funds."

The county argued that information given to voters during the campaign for the park propositions was not binding; "statements disseminated to the general public before a bond election . . . are not factors to be considered in determining the purpose for which bond issue funds . . . can be spent," it told the court.

Green disagreed. In a memo to the court opposing the county's request for dismissal of the lawsuit, he laid bare details of the county's behavior in the years since the propositions were approved—details that had only become known through depositions and discovery after the lawsuit was filed.

The support of the Open Space Council was, Green said, based on the "repeated promises of the defendants that the general obligation bonds would be used to acquire seven new park sites to be available to all people in the county, rich and poor alike, and that the taxpayers' money would not finance defendants' elaborate country club recreation facilities, which could clearly be used only by those persons sufficiently wealthy to pay the fees."

"Now, in 1972," he continued, "we find that the defendants are betraying the voters. The defendants have not acquired and do not plan to acquire the seven new park sites and three additional sites for recreation centers. On the contrary, the defendants deliberately purchased a smaller tract at the Queeny site than had been promised, saving approximately $600,000 of the money originally promised for land acquisition. In addition, the defendants have taken the $1,241,517 originally budgeted for acquisition of a site for a northwest county recreation center and transferred it from the land acquisition account to development accounts, and have decided not to purchase the promised site. Thus defendants have robbed the land acquisition funds of approximately $1.8 million. They have in addition persuaded two private donors to contribute $2,000,000. Putting these funds into one bundle, the defendants have approximately $3.8 million which they claim they can use in any way they see fit."

"With this money, together with a part of the proposed revenue bond issue, they now plan to build an elaborate Disneyland in the Queeny Park. This will include not merely an ice-skating hockey rink, but an elaborate arena seating 2,000 spectators, or 5,000 persons when the ice is put away. It will include one or more swimming pools, a golf course, tennis courts and other facilities. . . . Beyond that, defendants propose to pay for the operation and maintenance of this elaborate country club (other than the golf course) out of the Park Maintenance Fund, that is, the eight-cent ad valorem tax imposed upon all real estate in the county, thus keeping the gross revenues from the use of these facilities to pay off the revenue bonds. Finally, the defendants have promised prospective revenue bond purchasers that the county government will somehow, no matter what happens, operate and maintain all of the recreation centers, and if the revenues are not sufficient the county will make up any deficit from other funds available."

No longer did the plaintiffs seek to bar the county from selling the revenue bonds: "plaintiffs are inclined to the view that revenue bond purchasers may buy the proffered bonds at their own risk," Green wrote. However, the plaintiffs "are asking this court to enter a declaratory judgment as to the proper use of the proceeds of the general obligation bond sale and the revenue bond sale and to enjoin defendants from misappropriating the park maintenance fund or any other tax supported fund."

For, after being allowed to look at the prospectus given to the bond companies, Green and the plaintiffs had discovered that the county had used or was planning to use general obligation bond proceeds for "all costs of engineering and architectural fees" for the three recreational complexes (one of which was now being proposed for Queeny) and that it was pledging to use county funds for construction and operation of the ice rink and swimming pool at Queeny. In addition, none of the user fees generated would be applied to maintenance or costs of operating the facilities, but that the entire gross revenues of "all three golf, ice and swimming facilities" would be pledged to pay off the revenue bonds. Finally, the county was telling its bonders that if the user fees fell short of what was needed to pay off the bonds, "the county will make up any deficit from other funds available."

According to the prospectus, general obligation bonds and contributions (namely, from Mrs. Queeny and the Greensfelder Foundations) were already being used for development of facilities at Queeny Park: architectural and engineering fees totaling $265,000, equipment costing $200,000, and some $2.8 million for construction of the ice rink, swimming facilities, tennis courts, and an elaborate children's playground. The prospectus also stated that the county had encumbered $445,400 for the feasibility study and for architectural fees for the North and South County Recreation complexes—and for a golf course at Queeny Park.

All totaled, Green discovered, general obligation funds totaling $643,000 had been encumbered in support of the recreational facilities that voters had been told would be self-supporting. In addition, prospective bond purchasers were informed that all additional expenses needed for architectural and engineering services would be paid for from the same (non-revenue-bond) funds. "No charges will be made to the Revenue Bond proceeds for these services," the prospectus said.

In short, the county was telling prospective buyers of their revenue bonds that regardless of what kind of income was generated by the recreational facilities, the "full faith and honor of St. Louis County" would be pledged to pay off the bonds, even if it meant taking money from the county's park maintenance fund, financed by taxpayers.

A MIXED VERDICT

THE CASE BEFORE JUDGE SCHAAF WAS HEARD IN SEPTEMBER 1972. HIS DECISION, issued in February 1973, upheld the plaintiffs in their claim that the county should be barred from using funds other than income from the recreational facilities to pay off the revenue bonds. "The notice of sale and prospectus" issued by the county "does say that 'the county will make up any deficit from other funds available,'" the judge noted. "It is obvious this language should not have been used. It is not included in the ordinance . . . and further it violates the language" approved by the voters. "The county cannot use tax funds to pay off said revenue bonds but only the gross or net revenues of its park or recreation facilities or unrestricted gifts for park purposes."

On the matter of the county's withholding of documents from the public, the judge also upheld the plaintiffs, finding that they, as well as other citizens and taxpayers of St. Louis County, "have the right to inspect the feasibility study and prospectus."

But on other issues, the plaintiffs' claims were rejected. The revenue bonds, he determined, could be paid from either net or gross revenues from the facilities, as well as from gifts or grants from any source, including federal revenue-sharing funds. Also, county tax funds could be used to help pay operating expenses of Queeny Park, thus freeing more funds for repayment of the revenue bonds. Also, "the recreation center as now proposed may be built within the confines of Queeny Park," he ruled, despite the county's promise to acquire a new site specifically for that purpose.

As a final blow, Schaaf ruled that court costs would be taxed "one fourth against defendants and three-fourths against plaintiffs."

In October 1973, Green appealed Schaaf's decision to the Missouri Court of Appeals, St. Louis District. A year later, in August 1974, that court upheld Schaaf's decision, for the most part. On just one point did it rule in the plaintiffs' favor: it found that the county could not use proceeds from the general obligation bonds "to construct or develop swimming pools, skating/ice hockey rinks, or golf courses."

In November 1975, the Missouri Supreme Court issued its decision in the case. It did not agree that the county's decision to locate a recreational center in Queeny Park was contrary to law or to the ballot propositions approved in 1969. "The development of Queeny as proposed is within the scope of the propositions submitted and is a permissible development of the land acquired," the court found.

But on other points, the county was rebuffed. "The use of general obligation bond money is limited to the purposes for which it was voted," the court found. "Such money is similar to trust money. . . . We cannot ignore the fact that [two propositions] were submitted to the people together. . . . The ultimate question is what did the voters approve, and any doubts must be resolved in favor of the taxpayers.

"We conclude that the propositions as submitted did not contemplate the use of general obligation bond money to construct swimming pools, skating rinks, or golf courses. . . . The record . . . supports the

conclusion that revenue bonds were proposed because the facilities contemplated were of the type for which general taxpayer support is difficult
to achieve unless the cost is borne by those using the facilities. . . . The
publicity campaign, which is a part of the history of the election . . .
clearly indicated that the pools, rinks, and golf courses were to be built
with . . . money *at no cost to the taxpayer.* Funds from [the general obligation bonds] were not for those purposes and may not now be so used."

On the question of whether the county could use tax funds to operate or maintain the recreational facilities built with proceeds from the
revenue bonds during the life of the bonds, "Plaintiffs ask merely for a
declaratory judgment as to the validity and enforceability of this pledge
or obligation," arguing that this obligation of tax funds violated Article
VI, Section 26(a) of the Missouri Constitution. "We agree," the court
wrote. "An undertaking by the county to operate and maintain these facilities with its general revenue for the life of these bonds would create a
present indebtedness and obligate the county to levy taxes in subsequent
years for its payment."

The court refused to rule, however, that the county was out of bounds
in proposing to build a recreational center at Queeny, rather than at a
yet-to-be-purchased site. The lower court judgment that the recreational
center may be built at Queeny was affirmed.

"As a result of review by the court of appeals and by this court," the
justices wrote in their unanimous opinion, "plaintiffs have prevailed in
all but one of the major issues presented by them," and as such, were
entitled to recover "all the taxable costs." With that, the Supreme Court
remanded the case with instructions to the trial court judge to enter
judgment consistent with the high court's opinion.

ACCOUNTABILITY

FOR ANY OTHER ATTORNEY, THAT, PERHAPS, WOULD HAVE BEEN THE END OF THE
matter. But not for Green.

He had barely obtained the new lower court judgment (January 26,
1979), than he filed a motion to amend it, asking now for an accounting
of any and all expenditures of funds raised through the 1969 general
obligation bond proceeds.

In support of his motion, he filed the affidavit of the county's auditor, Ronald L. Young, who stated that a detailed audit would be needed to determine what expenditures had been made from the county fund—Fund 210—into which general obligation bond proceeds had been placed. "I have determined that since September 1972, substantial expenditures have been made from that fund to pay for the construction of the skating rink and swimming pool at Queeny Park," Young stated. "The present accounting system does not capture costs for rink and pool separately from other costs. Therefore, without a detailed audit it is not possible to determine the total amount of those expenditures. This could be done with a detailed audit."

His preliminary review, he said, suggested "that substantial expenditures were made from Fund 210 which appear to be contrary to the Supreme Court Decision. From this limited review I am unable to conclude whether those expenditures have been fully reimbursed."

When presiding Judge Robert G.J. Hoester announced he would not issue an order immediately, saying he was unsure of his jurisdiction in the case, Green returned to the Supreme Court, with a writ of mandamus, asking it to order the county to provide the accounting.

In late April 1979, the Supreme Court agreed, noting: "It now appears that St. Louis County may not have complied with the declaration issued by this court in its 1975 ruling. An accounting would demonstrate any such noncompliance and would render effective that decision."

In the briefs filed with the Supreme Court, all those made on behalf of Hoester were drawn up by the county's attorneys, who sought to defend his initial claim to lack jurisdiction.

In late 1980, the Supreme Court issued its second ruling in this case, finding that in fact, the lower court judge did have jurisdiction over the matters raised in Green's motion. "The trial court should not relax its grasp upon the *res* until it shall have avoided a multiplicity of suits by doing full, adequate, and complete justice between the parties," the court found. The victory was an empty one, however, since Hoester never did require the county to make the detailed accounting.

BATTLING THE PRESS

GREEN'S BATTLE IN THE COURTS LASTED THE BETTER PART OF A DECADE. AND WHILE it did not stop the county from developing Queeny Park in ways far beyond what the public was promised, the litigation did set clear limits on how the county could finance such projects.

Even after the last brief was filed, Green continued to lead efforts to protect Queeny Park and to thwack down, at every opportunity, the county's efforts to rewrite the history of the park, often with the collusion of lazy or incompetent reporters.

In 1985, for example, the St. Louis County Council approved an ordinance that gave a lease option to professional golfer Hale Irwin to develop a golf course at one or more of three county sites, including Queeny Park. A feature article on Irwin's plans by *St. Louis Post-Dispatch* reporter Steve Kelley included a few background paragraphs on the litigation, prompting Green to fire off a three-page-long letter to managing editor David Lipman.

Kelley's article stated that following the 1969 approval of the revenue bond issue by voters, "construction was stymied by a lawsuit contending that golf courses did not constitute proper use of park land. That obstacle was overcome in the courts. . . ."

But, as Green noted, "It is not true that construction was stymied by a lawsuit contending that golf courses did not constitute proper use of park land, and it is utterly untrue that 'that obstacle was overcome in the courts.'

"In fact, construction was stymied in the first instance by the simple fact that golf courses do not make enough money to support revenue bonds." Then the county tried to sell revenue bonds with a pledge to back them with county tax revenues, Green wrote: "Issuance of those misnamed revenue bonds, and therefore arguably 'construction,' was indeed thereafter stymied by a lawsuit. The Supreme Court ruled in 1975 that the county administration proposal was entirely illegal."

The revision of history was particularly troubling, Green wrote, in that, "in misleading the reader as to the facts, it distracts the reader from several real issues of public concern, which . . . should be publicly debated. For example, the county council, as well as the press and the public, should now be demanding a detailed feasibility study, which takes a hard look at the economics of a revenue bond issue to finance a golf course. . . . Other questions, also, should be debated by the public. In these times, is it appropriate to devote a massive expenditure of public resources (at least the acreage on which the golf courses would be located) to an activity in which only a small number of relatively prosperous citizens participate? Is it appropriate for the government to enter into competition with private golf course operators in St. Louis County? Is it appropriate to remove some of our prime, scarce park acreage from public use by large numbers of people for such purposes as picnicking, hiking, and general unstructured recreation, and turn it over to the exclusive use of relatively prosperous adults?

"I do not expect your sports writers to appreciate or raise these questions. But other persons should not be diverted from these questions by misstatements of this sort. The Post-Dispatch should do better by its readers."

But Green evidently had little faith that the *Post-Dispatch* would launch the type of discussion he wanted to see. The same day he wrote Lipman he also sent a letter to the three Democratic members of the County Council: Jerry Corcoran, Donald Bond, and Harry Von Romer.

"Some of you may recall that ten years ago, the three Democratic members of the St. Louis County Council were so concerned about the actions of the majority, and the opinion of the court of appeals, that they were moved to file their own separate brief in the Supreme Court, parting company with the majority of the council and the supervisor. . . . The concerns expressed in that brief are as valid today as they were at that time."

"At all times since 1972," Green told the council members, "the county administration has endeavored to cover up its own incompetence by mis-stating the facts, and all too often the press echoes those mis-statements." Green urged the council members to focus on the "real issues of public concern" that he described in the letter to Lipman.

Less than a month later, though, Green was again registering his complaints over revisionist history in the pages of the *Post-Dispatch*. The offending article this time was a news article by Margaret Gillerman, the newspaper's beat reporter for St. Louis County government.

The main thrust of Gillerman's article, published on April 21, 1985, was to note Green's objections to the county's deal with Hale Irwin. In a letter to Gillerman dated May 3, 1985, Green wrote: "The story under your byline . . . is almost as bad as the other stories the Post has printed on this subject. I realize that most of this is probably not your fault, because the editors in charge of the news department have been rewriting all stories on this subject for the last thirteen years, consistently misstating and misrepresenting the facts, in an effort to protect the image of former Supervisor Roos, while denigrating the efforts of the citizens who went to court to uphold the law."

Gillerman wrote that Green had filed suit in 1972 "on behalf of environmentalists who objected to using revenue bonds to finance golf courses."

Green wrote: "Your editors know very well, and my letter [to Lipman] which fell into your hands makes it very clear, that I did not file suit, on behalf of 'environmentalists' or anybody else, 'who objected to using revenue bonds to finance golf courses.' On the contrary, I contended on behalf of the plaintiffs in that case, and the Supreme Court ruled, that the county was explicitly authorized to issue revenue bonds, and only revenue bonds, to finance the construction of golf courses, and could not use general obligation bonds, falsely described as revenue bonds, for that purpose. Thus the Post continues its relentless, thirteen-year campaign to deceive the readers, by false statements."

Gillerman quoted Thomas Wehrle, the county attorney, as saying that Green's lawsuit "made the bonds unmarketable." This, Green said, "is true only in the sense (which the Post-Dispatch always conceals) that the lawsuit resulted in a Supreme Court ruling that the bonds which the county was attempting to market were unconstitutional. That ruling, not the lawsuit by itself, made the phony bonds unmarketable.

"While the Post-Dispatch has a constitutional right to print such nonsense . . . no responsible journal should print such nonsense without printing, along side it, the facts.

"I suppose the Post should be given some credit for belatedly making an effort to inform the reader of the ruling of the Supreme Court; that is more than the Post usually does. . . . On the other hand, the totally misleading statement of the court's ruling will mislead the reader more than would omission of the paragraph. . . . By and large, the less the Post news pages print, the less they mislead."

GOLF—AGAIN

THE HALE IRWIN GOLF COURSE OPTION EXPIRED, BUT IN JANUARY 1986, THE County Council voted 6–0 to approve a 20-year lease with another golf course operator, William S. Bahn and Bahn, Ortman, Inc., for a golf course either at the North County recreation center or at Queeny Park. Six months later, the council authorized the county supervisor to enter into a lease agreement with Bahn, Ortman for a golf course at Queeny Park.

By then, public opposition to developing a golf course at Queeny was in full flower, led by a group calling itself Friends for Natural Heritage Parks. Under county law, opponents of any ordinance passed by the council have 10 days within which to present a petition signed by at least 500 voters that puts an automatic 40-day hold on the legislation taking effect. If the opponents seek to put the ordinance up for a referendum vote, they need to then collect 24,000 signatures within that 40-day period.

The 500 signatures were easily collected, and the group also had no trouble meeting the 24,000-signature threshold for putting the ordinance on the referendum ballot. In addition, the group proposed a referendum calling for protection of Natural Heritage Parks within St. Louis County. Parks so designated would be off-limits to golf courses, ball parks, recreation centers, and the like.

The county administration opposed both measures. It authorized a budget of $50,000 to finance a public relations campaign against them— which was immediately challenged by the Friends for Natural Heritage Parks.

By the time a judge barred the county from further expenditures from the fund, in October, all but $272 had been spent.

That November, both propositions won approval of the voters, by an overwhelming margin.

CHAPTER 2

DESPITE SUPREME COURT VICTORY, A SETBACK FOR CLEAN AIR STANDARDS

Patricia Tummons

FOR SIX YEARS, UNION ELECTRIC, THE UTILITY PROVIDING POWER TO THE ST. LOUIS region, was the *bête noire* of Lewis Green. The range of arenas in which the two tangled descended from the sublime to the ridiculous: from the lofty reaches of the U.S. Supreme Court, where Green saw his views vindicated in an early go-round, to the burlesque of hearings before the Missouri Air Conservation Commission.

In the end, Green never was able to force the utility to comply with the sulfur dioxide emission limits that the Missouri Air Conservation Commission adopted in 1967, when Green was at its helm. But he was able to achieve a stunning legal victory in the Supreme Court, one that set the tone for implementation of the Clean Air Act for years to come.

NO ALBATROSS

IT ALL STARTED IN MAY OF 1974. THE ENVIRONMENTAL PROTECTION AGENCY had notified Union Electric that emissions of sulfur dioxide from three coal-burning plants—at Labadie, Portage des Sioux, and Meramec—had exceeded the amounts allowed under the federally approved state implementation plan for the St. Louis Metropolitan Area. In August, UE appealed to the 8th U.S. Circuit Court of Appeals, seeking review of the sulfur dioxide rule, with which, UE claimed, the three plants could not possibly comply (although the Meramec plant eventually did).

27

Green's involvement began in November of that year when, on behalf of the Missouri Coalition for the Environment, he petitioned the 8th U.S. Circuit Court of Appeals for leave to file an *amicus* brief in the case.

At the heart of the state implementation plan for control of sulfur dioxide was Regulation 10, adopted by the Air Conservation Commission in 1967, when Green was its chairman. The regulation limited sulfur dioxide emissions from power plants to a maximum of 2.3 pounds for each million British thermal units (BTU) of output. According to UE, the regulation was more stringent than what was needed to attain the national standard and, in any case, the technology to achieve reductions on this scale was not available.

UE's claim was dismissed on March 27, 1975, by the appeals court, which noted in its opinion that it had adopted the standard of review recommended by the Coalition in its *amicus* brief. The Clean Air Act allowed state implementation plans to be appealed within 30 days of their approval, with appeals outside that time frame limited only to cases in which grounds for appeal rose after the appeal deadline had passed. And although the technological and economic considerations raised by UE "are important ones needing resolution," the appeals court decision held, "they are not appropriate for judicial resolution but are essentially legislative judgments as to where the public interest lies."

In June, UE appealed to the U.S. Supreme Court, which agreed to hear the case.

Again Green filed an *amicus* brief on behalf of the Coalition. The utility, he wrote, "has coexisted peacefully (more or less) with Missouri's Regulation 10 since March 24, 1967, by invoking the variance procedure. ... Time and again, [UE] has renewed its variance."

Why, then, Green asked in the brief, was the utility now seeking to void the rule, when it could just as easily have asked for another variance? Indeed, Green pointed out, UE had an application to renew its variance pending before the Air Conservation Commission when it appealed the regulation to the 8th Circuit in 1974. He then answered his own question: "Apparently [UE] looked apprehensively at the approaching date of May 31, 1975; for periods after that date, the Eighth Circuit (like the First, Second, and Fifth) had shot down the variance procedure. ... This foreboding generated the spectre of gloom and doom which haunts the petition for review, and which was trotted out before the court of appeals."

Yet in April 1975, just a month after the 8th Circuit Court had issued its judgment in the UE case, the Supreme Court had ruled (*Train v. NRDC*) that variances of the sort issued in Missouri were perfectly legal, so long as they did not interfere with states' attainment of clean air standards.

With the *Train* decision now the law of the land, Green argued, UE's appeal of Regulation 10 made no sense. "To play out the remainder of this litigation before this Court now, after *Train v. NRDC* resuscitated the variance procedure . . . is like playing out *The Rime of the Ancient Mariner* without the albatross," he wrote. "There is no reason to suppose that petitioner and the Missouri Air Conservation Commission cannot continue to find an accommodation satisfactory to them and to the Environmental Protection Agency."

But what UE wanted was more than a variance from the rule: it wanted to knock Regulation 10 out of the ballpark altogether, arguing that the rule went further than what the federal Clean Air Act required. The appeals court had refused to do that for a number of reasons. When the Supreme Court agreed to take the case on appeal, it narrowed the question down to just one point: Did the Clean Air Act open the window to appeals of state implementation plans on the basis of technological and economic factors after the 30-day window for appeals had closed and when (1) those same factors made it impossible for the utility to comply and (2) it was "manifestly against the public interest for it to attempt to do so."

The utility argued to the court that it could not have known at the time the state plan was approved that meeting it would be technologically and economically impossible. It asked for relief in the form of an order that the 8th Circuit appoint a master to hear evidence and make findings that would then be reviewed by the appeals court.

Green, who was well aware of the objections raised by UE when Regulation 10 was adopted, disputed the utility's claim that it did not know of the technological and economic challenges that the rule imposed at the time it was adopted as part of the state implementation plan. On January 5, 1972, at a public hearing on the adoption of the plan, Green wrote, UE Vice President Earl Dille said, "If the people of this metropolitan area want to spend a quarter of a billion dollars to reduce anticipated ground-level SO_2 concentrations in the vicinity of Labadie from .0024 parts per million to .0004 parts per million, it is their decision to make." As for the claim that the rule was more stringent than what was needed for St. Louis to achieve national air quality standards for sulfur dioxide, Green wrote, it was irrelevant. Even assuming that the claim was correct, it would not be grounds for disapproval by the EPA administrator. If the plan is sufficient to meet federal standards, the Clean Air Act stated, the administrator "*shall* approve such plan," Green wrote, quoting the provision in the act.

In any event, Green argued in the *amicus* brief, Missouri's standard for sulfur dioxide was not based on technology but on air quality, leaving it up to the power-plant operators to decide how they should meet it. "Missouri . . . has been careful to draw up its regulations in terms of *performance,* leaving the industrial sources free to use whatever means they think best to achieve the required reduction (if any) of emissions. . . . The utilities are free to choose any method they desire to achieve that maximum. . . . Thus, it cannot rationally be argued that, because of economic or technological difficulties, Missouri should have devised some alternative regulation for large power plants."

Justice Thurgood Marshall delivered the Supreme Court's opinion on June 25, 1976. Marshall noted that the 1970 amendments to the Clean Air Act give each state "wide discretion" in formulating its plan to meet clean air standards, and that the plan is to be approved by the EPA "if it has been adopted after public notice and hearing and if it meets eight specified criteria."

It was the position of the EPA that the Clean Air Act does not give the administrator authority to reject a plan on the ground of economic or technological infeasibility, "and we have previously accorded great deference to the administrator's construction of the Clean Air Act," Marshall wrote. "After surveying the relevant provisions of the Clean Air Act Amendments of 1970 and their legislative history, we agree that Congress intended claims of economic and technological infeasibility to be wholly foreign to the administrator's consideration of a state implementation plan."

"Technology forcing," he continued, referring to the idea that air standards can force the development of technology when such technology does not exist at the time the standards are adopted, "is a concept somewhat new to our national experience and it necessarily entails certain risks. But Congress considered those risks in passing the 1970 amendments and decided that the dangers posed by uncontrolled air pollution made them worth taking."

Ongoing Violations

In September 1976, two months after the Supreme Court rebuff, UE petitioned the Missouri Air Conservation Commission, seeking to change Regulation 10. It was prevented from seeking a variance, it argued, because EPA regulations called for variances to be made a part of the state implementation plan with an appropriate showing of eventual compliance. And UE, claiming it could never comply, could not meet that requirement. The air commission took no action.

A year later, in September 1977, UE asked the Air Conservation Commission for variances from Regulation 10 for its plants, variances that would allow it to emit up to 6.3 pounds of sulfur dioxide per million BTU at Labadie and up to 7.3 pounds per million BTU at Sioux. In addition, the petition requested modification of Missouri's state implementation plan to include the variances, if they should be approved. The utility claimed that the EPA had essentially invited it to take this step when a representative of the agency's regional office stated in an April meeting of the commission that variances could be approved even absent an accompanying compliance schedule. The commission did not grant the variances, but instead scheduled the petitions for hearing early the following year.

Before then, however, the EPA carried out inspections of the Meramec, Sioux, and Labadie plants and found air pollution violations at all three, with the Sioux and Labadie plants exceeding sulfur dioxide emission limitations. On January 13, 1978, the EPA served UE with the notice of violation, ordering the violations to cease within 30 days, and threatening penalties of up to $50,000 for each day of violation after that.

Union Electric was back in court on February 9, asking Judge Roy Harper of the U.S. Court for Missouri's Eastern District for a preliminary and permanent injunction barring the EPA from taking any enforcement action. While the company intended to comply with opacity regulations, it could not do so in the 30-day period the EPA was requiring, lawyers for the company stated. And with respect to the sulfur dioxide violations, "we allege and will prove that it is an utter impossibility for the company to comply." In addition to claiming (as it had before the Supreme Court) that the state standard was higher than it needed to be to achieve national standards, UE also argued that meeting the state standards would impose a financial hardship. "Aside from shutting down the plants, the only way the SO_2 emission regulation could be met at those plants would be by installation of flue gas desulfurization (FGD) equipment or the use of low sulfur coal," it told the court. In the first instance, installing the equipment, known as scrubbers, would take up to five years and require $713,316,000 in addition to annual recurring costs of $137,527,000—an amount that the utility said it could not possibly raise. Using low sulfur coal would add about $178,980,000 a year, plus a capital investment of $49,000,000, UE said, resulting in a rate increase of 25 percent—supposing it could even find a sufficient supply of low sulfur coal.

On March 16, 1978, Judge Harper granted the injunction, pending resolution of UE's petitions to change the state standards.

Meanwhile, at MACC

On January 9, 1978, John Levis, chairman of the Missouri Air Conservation Commission, wrote then-state Attorney General John Ashcroft concerning the upcoming hearings on the UE variance request.

The commission, Levis wrote, "because of the tremendous amount of public interest and testimony connected with the case, feels that an adversary hearing should be held so that all relevant facts can be presented in a public forum. . . . The Air Conservation Commission finds itself about to hold a hearing without counsel to represent the public to extrapolate appropriate evidence or cross examine witnesses. . . . I hereby formally request of you . . . that a qualified attorney be appointed for this specific hearing."

On January 17, Ashcroft responded: "This office has interrogated the departmental staff in order to assure ourselves that the concerns of the public have been and will continue to be safeguarded. . . . I have instructed [deputy attorney general] Dan Summers to be vigilant to the informational needs of the commission and to interject himself into the proceedings at any point where it appears that arguably relevant evidence is not being presented, where evidence is being distorted for any reason, or where the method of presenting evidence could lead to ambiguities."

Summers, however, was the deputy assigned to represent the Missouri Department of Natural Resources, which had already recommended that UE's petition for variances be granted.

When the commission met on January 18, 1978, members pressed Summers on how he proposed to represent the public's interest as well as the DNR's. "I have assured myself, from my knowledge of the situation and environmental law in general, that the department's recommendation is, in fact, on solid ground, whether or not everyone agrees with that recommendation," Summers said.

Commission chairman John Levis then asked the head of the DNR's Air Quality Division, Michael Marshall, "When you made your recommendations to the department director to adopt the variance in question, what did you supply the department director with on which to have her base her judgment to either make the recommendation or to deny the recommendation?"

Marshall replied, "It was a verbal discussion of the findings of the staff and accompanied by a written—a memorandum, interoffice memorandum, on the staff's conclusions of the review of the variance application."

Levis asked whether the memorandum reflected independent analysis by DNR staff or was based on material provided by UE. Marshall then was forced to acknowledge no memorandum actually existed—that, instead, he had only passed on his recommendation to someone on the director's staff.

Under further questioning from Levis, Marshall conceded that his staff had developed no information on the variance request and relied on information provided by UE.

"So, . . . really, what we have in front of us is merely the evidence which was submitted by the petitioner?" Levis asked.

Marshall did not want to concede the point. "There are several documents in the files . . . that were reviewed by the staff independent of UE's petition and support material."

But Levis and other commissioners were not convinced. John

Barsanti asked Marshall if he felt his staff was competent to make an economic analysis and assess the technological issues in the UE case.

Marshall replied, "I honestly cannot report that capability at the present time" to review the technological issues. With respect to economic questions, "I don't think the staff, to my mind, ever had the capability" of doing a detailed analysis, he said.

When it turned out that UE had filed a supplemental petition with the DNR the previous day, recalculating its estimate of emissions under the variances it sought among other things, commissioners were even more put out with Marshall.

"Why were we not informed of this last night?" Chairman Levis asked. "We met on this very subject for last night for two and a half hours, all right? At no time was this mentioned."

The best Marshall could respond was, "I was planning to send you the additional information."

In March, the commission held a two-day hearing on the variance petition sought by UE. The Coalition for the Environment, represented by Green, had been granted status as a party to the case. Green called UE's vice president of power operations, John McLaughlin, to testify as an "adverse witness."

"Is it your understanding that the company is requesting this commission to prescribe an emission rate which is substantially the same as what is now being emitted from each of those two plants?" Green asked.

"That is correct," McLaughlin answered.

THE FINAL ACT

IN JULY 1978, THE AIR CONSERVATION COMMISSION ISSUED ITS DECISION TO GRANT the variance, to be in effect until such time as clean air standards are themselves changed or the power plants are able to comply with the standards.

Within the month, litigation commenced again—this time, in the Circuit Court of Cole County, Missouri (in Jefferson City). On August 25, the Coalition for the Environment sued the commission; six days later, the state of Illinois sued as well. Illinois's concern was that the commission did not take into account the impact of the variance on Illinois. If sulfur dioxide emissions on the Missouri side of the Mississippi continued at the rate allowed in the variance, Illinois's air quality would be diminished to the point that economic growth would be curtailed, it claimed. The commission's findings of fact "made it clear that it did not consider in its deliberations the impact of sources in either Illinois or Missouri on the air quality and potential industrial growth of the other state," its attorney general claimed. Since the March hearings, studies on this very point had been completed and received, Illinois noted, asking the court to remand the matter to the commission for further deliberations.

The studies, conducted by Environmental Research and Technology (ERT) and released in September 1978, showed that air pollution regulations in Missouri and Illinois were not stringent enough to meet federal air quality standards for suspended particulates (soot and dust, for the most part) and sulfur dioxide.

But eclipsing the litigation and concerns over air quality were the Clean Air Act Amendments of 1977. One of the provisions made it impossible for any major stationary source—including, especially, any power plant—to continue to operate under variances after July 1, 1979. The owner of any plant not meeting state regulations by that time would face a "non-compliance penalty," assessed automatically and equivalent to the amount of money saved by non-compliance. In the case of the Sioux and Labadie plants, UE estimated that the penalties could amount to $140 million per year.

Once more, UE was back before the Air Conservation Commission, seeking to relax Regulation 10 to the point that the two big St. Louis plants could be in compliance without the company having to install scrubbers or burn exclusively more expensive low sulfur coal. The company proposed that the Labadie plant be allowed to emit 6.3 pounds per million BTU and that the Sioux plant be allowed to emit 7.3 pounds per million BTU—four and five pounds, respectively, over the 2.3 pounds allowed in Regulation 10. After December 31, 1981, the proposed emission limits would be lowered somewhat, though still not to the 2.3 pound limit of Regulation 10. In addition, UE proposed that both plants would be allowed to emit up to 20 percent more than the standards allowed for three days a month.

In October 1978, the Air Conservation Commission published a proposed revision to Regulation 10 that would effectively make the emissions allowed in the variances the new standard for sulfur dioxide emissions from the Sioux and Labadie plants. At a hearing on the proposed relaxed rule in December 1978, public opinion was overwhelmingly opposed.

In an apparent effort to mollify its critics, UE released a statement noting that, "although the revisions are technically a 'relaxation' of the federally approved emissions limitations . . . the plants have in fact been operating at a higher level of emissions under a series of state-issued variances. . . . [T]he submitted 'relaxations' will in fact result in a significant <u>reduction</u> of SO_2 emissions from the plants." In addition, UE Vice President Earl Dille informed the Air Conservation Commission in January that "the company has reluctantly agreed with the EPA and the staff of the Missouri Department of Natural Resources to support a 4.8 [pound per million BTU] emission standard at both Labadie and Sioux, in order to ensure that EPA approval, which is absolutely essential, will be forthcoming."

The Coalition for the Environment registered its strong objections: "Even if the modeling studies submitted by Union Electric in fact demonstrated what they purport to demonstrate, they would not succeed in demonstrating that the proposed regulation will not result in short-term violations to the ambient air quality standards in the vicinity of the Labadie and Sioux plants. . . . The proposed regulation allows emissions up to 5.75 [pounds per million BTU], three days per month. As far as the Coalition has been able to determine, there is no model which shows that emissions at [this level] will not result in short-term violations. The presumption is the contrary, since 4.8 appears to be the highest number which Enviroplan [UE's consultant] can put into its computer without generating violations."

The Coalition's objections were for naught. The final regulation, which differed in few significant respects from what UE had proposed, was adopted in early 1979 and the variances were no longer needed. In February 1979, the 8th U.S. Circuit Court of Appeals, where the EPA had appealed the injunction issued against enforcement of clean air standards, overturned Judge Harper's decision at the District Court level, but by then, with the changed standards having been adopted, enforcement was a moot issue. In July 1980, the Cole County Circuit Court, on motion of the plaintiffs, dismissed the joined appeals of the variances brought by the Coalition for the Environment and Illinois.

Chapter 3

Fighting Against Long Odds to Halt a Nuclear Power Plant at Callaway

Patricia Tummons

"Litigation is not for the faint of heart." So wrote Lewis Green in a letter to clients that discussed a possible settlement of their lawsuit. He continued:

> We didn't start this suit to run away from it when it heats up. There is a real possibility of accomplishing something worthwhile. As self-appointed custodians of the public welfare, we have assumed a responsibility. The public is entitled to have the law enforced. As long as there is a realistic possibility of enforcing it, we owe the public the effort.

Those few sentences neatly wrap up Green's approach to practically every case he took on. So long as there remained a glimmer of hope that the particular cause he was championing could yet prevail, Green stuck with it. Challenges that other attorneys might have dismissed as quixotic or doomed were Green's meat and potatoes.

But the years of legal battles over the planned Callaway nuclear plant must have drained even Green.

REACTORS ON THE MISSOURI RIVER

IN 1973, UNION ELECTRIC CO., THE UTILITY SUPPLYING POWER TO MUCH OF central and eastern Missouri, hopped on the nuclear bandwagon and placed an order for two reactors, which it planned to build near Fulton, in Callaway County, five miles from the Missouri River. UE was a late-comer to the trend, which by then had already slowed considerably, with utilities elsewhere having begun to cancel reactor orders placed in the 1960s.

The following year, UE applied to the Nuclear Regulatory Commission for a permit to build the two reactors. The Missouri Coalition for the Environment, with Green as its attorney, intervened in the NRC hearings on the application. Among other things, it challenged UE's financial ability to undertake such an expensive project, whose cost, for both reactors, was said to run just over a billion dollars.

The NRC rejected the Coalition's challenge and granted UE the construction permit on April 16, 1976. By then, the Missouri Public Service Commission (PSC) had issued a decision allowing the utility to fold into its electric rates the costs associated with plant construction well before the reactors were in operation, and the utility had informed the PSC it was planning to add nearly a billion dollars to its rates to finance the project.

Within a year, opponents of the Callaway plant had collected enough signatures on an initiative petition to place a proposition—Proposition 1—before Missouri voters. By a two-to-one vote, the proposition became law, prohibiting electric utilities from folding construction costs into the rate base before power plants became "fully operational and used for service."

That was hardly the end of it.

In 1979, when the PSC opened a docket on Union Electric's program to expand its power-producing capability, Missourians for Safe Energy and the Coalition, both represented by Green, were admitted as parties to the case, as was the Missouri Office of the Public Counsel, the Department of Natural Resources, and, of course, the utility. The PSC had ordered the investigation on its own, after its staff had questioned the utility's forecasting methods and had noted that the utility's projections of peak demand had had to be revised downward consistently since 1973. Green's clients were vitally interested in this issue: if energy conservation were promoted as aggressively as consumption, then perhaps there would be no need for the utility to expand production capacity, including construction of the second Callaway reactor, which by then was on hold.

Transcripts of hearings in the case, held in the spring of 1980, when the first Callaway reactor was about 60 percent complete, run into the thousands of pages. The written testimony of the respective parties' experts filled dozens of binders. File drawers in the Green basement bulge with statements and pleadings, motions in support and opposition, rebuttals and surrebuttals.

One of the most critical witnesses presented by the utility was a computer modeler whose written testimony stated that his work supported the utility's planned expansion, including not just Callaway I and II, but also a third reactor at Callaway by 1994. Under cross-examination by Green, however, the witness said that the information on which his testimony was based had been destroyed. What's more, Green got the witness, Gilbert Elliott, to acknowledge that his computer simulations were based only on information fed to him by the utility, which biased the results. Had the utility given him a lower reserve capacity requirement (say, 15 to 18 percent reserve capacity requirement instead of the inflated 37 percent that UE said was needed), would Elliott's computer model have forecasted a need for the second reactor? Green asked.

"No," Elliott replied.

Green: If you had constrained the . . . model to a range of 15 to 25 percent, would it have selected Callaway II?

Elliott: I'd have to review that, but probably not.

Green: In fact, if you had given the . . . model the choice, rather than imposing Callaway I as a given, . . . it wouldn't have chosen Callaway I, either, would it?

Elliott: That would have been too narrow of a tunnel constraint for the . . . program.

Green: That means the answer is, it would not have chosen it.

Elliott: It would not have chosen it.

In October 1980, the parties filed their closing briefs. In his, Green questioned the utility's demand forecasts, noting that they had fudged actual historical usage in order to bolster the case for the Callaway reactors. "While other utilities are canceling nuclear plants right and left, UE has no interest in their reasoning and plunges blindly ahead with Callaway I and Callaway II. . . . [T]his conservation idea was put back on the shelf, apparently, permanently," he wrote. Although the PSC may have granted UE permission to build the reactors, "then the statute authorizing such issuance by implication authorizes its revocation, and it should now be revoked. . . . The company should be ordered, or at least encouraged, to cancel the Callaway project forthwith. . . . No more money, arguably to be recovered from the consumers, should be poured down the nuclear rat-hole."

The Missouri Office of Public Counsel was only slightly more moderate, recommending that the decision to terminate or continue construction of Callaway I should be left with management of the utility. "The consequences of management's decision . . . should be reviewed in detail when the company requests permission to add the completed plant to the rate base," Public Counsel William Barvick wrote in his summary of the case. With respect to the second Callaway reactor, he said, "The commission should order an immediate termination. . . . It should further direct the company to review alternative ways of meeting future demand, including but not limited to the construction of smaller plants, load management, rate design and conservation."

The PSC's own staff harshly criticized the utility's demand forecasts: "The staff contends that the company has not chosen tools suited to the best interest of its customers nor its stockholders. The company has chosen tools that justify past decisions rather than predict the best answers for the changing patterns the future will certainly bring. . . . Not only has the company prejudiced its forecasting methodology by the implicit exclusion of such long-term conservation programs as load management, but further, the persons who chose the forecasting variables and methodology have demonstrated error in judgment." The PSC staff went on to recommend that the PSC push the utility to submit revised demand forecasts and capacity models, updated construction budgets for Callaway, and a long-range plan to reduce demand by 25 percent, among other things. "These documents should be submitted within nine months in order to avoid assigning the risk of further construction on [Callaway] Unit 2. The commission cannot ignore the equity that is due future ratepayers. The commission cannot allow the Union Electric Company to postpone its day of reckoning."

FORECLOSED OPTIONS

DESPITE THE URGENT TONE IN ITS OWN STAFF'S WARNINGS, TWO YEARS LATER, THE Public Service Commission had still not issued any decision. By then, the utility had dropped plans to build the second Callaway reactor, while construction costs for the first one continued to rise, far beyond anything anticipated at the time of the 1980 hearings.

In September 1982, Green wrote to the commission, asking for an "expedited" decision and calling the commission's attention to a news release that UE had issued the previous month. "Direct costs" of Callaway I, the press release said, had increased to $1.8 billion from $1.4 billion, while carrying charges had risen to $1.05 billion from $700 million. Total costs rose from $2.1 billion to $2.85 billion.

"The numbers are a little confusing," Green wrote, "because none of them seems to match the numbers we were furnished before. Neither the $2.1 billion nor the $1.4 billion, established as the basis for comparison in the press release, matches the cost estimates furnished in the hearing or any revision to those cost estimates we have been able to make."

"The commission can learn from this experience," Green said. "The testimony offered by Union Electric in this case was preposterous when it was offered. It has now proved to be totally incorrect. The commission should learn to treat any testimony offered by the company as suspect and to pay attention to testimony and briefs presented by parties representing the public interest."

The commission, mute as Uncle Remus' Tar Baby, took no formal notice of Green's protest.

In May 1983, more than three years after the commission first heard arguments in the case, Green asked for the opportunity to brief the commission anew on aspects of the costs and financing of Callaway I as well as UE's new demand forecasts. He cited also a recent U.S. Supreme Court decision upholding the right of the state of California to stop construction of nuclear plants on the basis of economic reasons.

Instead, within days of Green's motion, the PSC issued an order saying only that UE had done a poor job of projecting future electrical demand and asking it and Kansas City Power & Light Co., which was building a nuclear reactor at Wolf Creek (a twin design of the Callaway plant), to brief the commission by June 30 on the question raised by the Supreme Court decision as to the commission's authority to halt or restrict completion of the two reactors under construction. UE was chastised for "an apparent lack of commitment to conservation techniques" but company officials were unbowed. "Even without seeing the order, we can say we will go ahead with construction of the Callaway plant," a UE spokesman told the *St. Louis Post-Dispatch.*

A Way Out

In 1984, as Callaway Unit I neared completion, a group called the Electric Ratepayers' Protection Project (ERPP) began collecting signatures on an initiative petition to put before Missouri voters a ballot measure that would establish the Electric Ratepayers' Protection Act. ERPP, a coalition of advocates for people with low incomes, church groups, legislators, anti-nuclear and civil rights activists that had come together two years earlier, warned in its brochures, "Huge rate hikes will hit customers of Union Electric and Kansas City Power & Light when their nuclear power plants go 'on line.'" "UE wants customers to pay a 70 percent rate increase over five years (25 percent the first year) for its Callaway plant. KCP&L will need at least a 50 percent rate increase for the Wolf Creek plant," the group claimed.

ERPP noted the enormous cost overruns—Unit I at Callaway was now estimated to cost five times the $550 million of initial forecasts— and warned they could go even higher. The power that Callaway and

Wolf Creek reactors would generate was not needed, costs of disposal of radioactive wastes were unknown, and the expenses of operating and maintaining nuclear plants could only increase as the plants aged.

The measure that ERPP proposed, drafted with Green's help, would have phased in rate hikes larger than 10 percent over several years. Costs not "just and reasonable" could not be included in the rate base. The proposed law would also give the commission the right to disallow "all or part of the cost of any unit" if the PSC held it to be "the result of poor management practices," unnecessary, or represented excess capacity.

One provision in the law would have prevented cost recovery for any nuclear reactor until a geological repository for the high-level nuclear waste created by such reactors had been developed. Even then, any rate increase would be subject to review by the state Legislature.

But the proposition also gave Union Electric and Kansas City Power & Light a way out, should they want to abandon their nuclear projects. If utilities with reactors under construction began dismantling them, they could ask the PSC to recover a "just and reasonable portion of the net after-tax losses" incurred, with the costs to the ratepayers phased in over a number of years, if necessary to prevent rate shock.

In July 1984, ERPP submitted the petition, with more than 84,000 signatures—twice the number required—to Missouri's secretary of state, James C. Kirkpatrick. Kirkpatrick then certified the petition, clearing the way for it to be put to voters in the November general election.

Union Electric sued, claiming that the measure would actually amend Missouri's constitution (in that it would require legislative rather than judicial review of PSC decisions). As such, the utility argued, ERPP should have had to collect thousands more signatures—8 percent of registered voters as opposed to 5 percent—to get the proposition on the ballot.

On September 14, the case was heard in Jefferson City by Circuit Judge Byron L. Kinder. Four days later, having found UE's arguments persuasive, Kinder ordered Kirkpatrick to remove the initiative from the ballot, finding that there were insufficient signatures for a constitutional amendment and also that the title of the proposition—"A Proposed Act Respecting Electrical Corporations"—was not legally sufficient. At the same time, Kinder stayed enforcement of his order until October 27, to allow for appeals.

ERPP immediately appealed the order to the Missouri Supreme Court, which referred it to the Court of Appeals, Western District. There, Green argued that it was premature to challenge Kirkpatrick's acceptance of it as a statute and not a constitutional amendment until after the vote. UE also appealed, claiming Kinder did not resolve its argument that the proposition was defective in other regards and, what's more, was pre-empted by federal laws.

On October 5, the appellate court affirmed Judge Kinder's decision. At the time the petition was submitted, the secretary of state should have reviewed the proposition to determine whether it was a statute or a constitutional amendment, the court found. "It is abundantly clear," the court continued, "that under [Article V, Section 18 of the Missouri Constitution], decisions of the Public Service Commission are subject only to judicial, and not legislative, review." The proposed statute "clearly constitutes a departure" from the Constitution, the court found.

The Supreme Court then heard the matter. On October 24, up against the deadline for ballots to be printed, it released its decision, reversing the lower courts and ordering the proposition to be taken to the voters. The decisions of the lower courts, the Supreme Court justices wrote in a 4–2 decision, were "contrary to a long line of decisions wherein we have held that, barring exceptional circumstances, we will not look beyond the face of the petition to determine its constitutionality prior to its being voted on by the electorate."

"Permits Charging Consumers . . ."

THE UTILITIES WERE BATTLING PROPOSITION B NOT ONLY IN THE COURTS, BUT also on the hustings, with a slick public relations campaign that was as expensive as it was dishonest. "No on B," the campaign drive set up by a newly formed group, Missourians Against Irresponsible Government, to gin up opposition to the proposition, had already raised more than a million dollars by the time Judge Kinder issued the first of the court rulings. By November 1, it was reporting to the secretary of state that it had received contributions of $3.1 million (with UE the largest single contributor). Other utilities across the state had given generously, as had national nuclear engineering and construction firms Bechtel and Daniel.

According to the *St. Louis Post-Dispatch,* spending by the group "has set a national record for an initiative on nuclear power and appears to be on the way to setting a national record for spending on all initiatives related to electric utilities." Final reports put total spending by the "No on B" campaign at more than $3.9 million.

By contrast, ERPP had raised just over $100,000, with Leo Drey the largest single donor ($34,477) and Lew Green having contributed $20,000 worth of legal services.

Not only did the utilities hold a towering advantage in fund-raising, but they also had as an ally the state attorney general (and Republican candidate for governor), John Ashcroft. At that time, Missouri law gave the attorney general the ability to write his own ballot titles (summaries that would be the only language voters would have to guide them in the ballot booth), without regard to the wishes of the people who had advanced them.

Ashcroft, no fan of the proposition, made the most of this prerogative.

His 35-word summary could not have been more inflammatory, leading off as it did by stating the measure "permits charging consumers for certain costs of electrical plants abandoned due to lack of approved waste disposal or other causes." Language that Green offered emphasized the benefits to ratepayers: "Limits electrical corporations' rate increases; prohibits charges for unjustified cost overruns, unneeded capacity, other companies' accidents, and nuclear plants without approved waste disposal process; requires cost sharing on abandonment of construction; prohibits evasion of regulation."

Ken Rothman, the Democratic candidate for governor, was quoted as saying Ashcroft's ballot language "could have come out of the Union Electric boardroom."

Although the proposition was supported with strong editorials in papers across the state, on November 6, the measure was overwhelmingly defeated. Voters rejected it by a 7 to 3 margin. According to Kay Drey, after the election, "Many people expressed disappointment, saying that the ballot wording had confused them."

CALLAWAY MOVES FORWARD

IN DECEMBER 1984, JUST SIX WEEKS AFTER THE VOTE, UNION ELECTRIC FILED notice with the Public Service Commission that the Callaway reactor was ready to go on-line. That was the milestone that would trigger a rate increase under a request that the utility had filed with the Public Service Commission earlier that year, seeking to recover construction costs of $2,987,248,000 associated with Callaway I.

The Coalition for the Environment and ERPP had, naturally, intervened in the rate case. In the petition to intervene, filed in March 1984, Green referred to the commission's 1980 hearings on the earlier docket dealing with the utility's capacity planning, where questions had arisen over the utility's judgment in pursuing Callaway. "The Coalition has been raising these issues before this commission for four years," Green wrote, "and has been attempting to persuade this commission to arrive at decisions on these issues, with no success.... The Coalition plans to raise these issues again, and to urge this commission to reach a decision."

But when Green asked that the entire record in the 1980 case be added to the record in the rate case, the commission wanted no part of it. Questions of excess capacity, of needless construction, of the utility's failure to pursue conservation—all went unaddressed in the rate case.

By late March 1985, the Public Service Commission, which had earlier been so painfully slow to address the utility's load management and prudence in construction of new plants, had reached its decision. It determined that roughly $400 million of the Callaway-related expenses "should not be recovered from ratepayers since they represent inefficient, imprudent, unreasonable or unexplained costs." It also rapped the utility's knuckles for failing to reassess its capacity plan "with regard to the economics of completing Callaway I" and noted, "UE never seriously considered other options once it began construction on Callaway.... The coal versus nuclear studies used by UE appear to have been specifically designed to justify the nuclear option already undertaken, rather than to objectively evaluate the nuclear plant in relation to other generation expansion alternatives.... UE should have known that its coal versus nuclear studies were not realistic and reliable." But in the end, it allowed UE to add $2,013,361,000 in costs associated with Callaway to the Missouri rate base.

The Last Card

Despite the setback, Green had not yet given up on the effort to stop the operation of Callaway Unit I. One last hand remained in play before the U.S. Court of Appeals for the District of Columbia Circuit. At issue was whether the Nuclear Regulatory Commission had improperly decided to disregard a utility's financial health in judging its fitness to run a nuclear reactor.

Starting in the early 1970s, many of the utilities planning and building nuclear reactors began to experience significant financial problems. Under existing regulations, the NRC could and did take a hard look at how those problems could affect a utility's ability to take on the expensive responsibility of operating a nuclear plant. Opponents of nuclear energy also used utilities' financial problems as a basis for challenging requests for licenses pending before the NRC.

But on March 31, 1982, the NRC eliminated that rule, holding that regulated utilities could recover the funds needed for safe construction of nuclear reactors and that no demonstrated link existed between financial qualifications and safety.

Opponents sued the NRC, and in February 1984 the U.S. Court of Appeals for the District of Columbia Circuit agreed with the plaintiffs. It found no merit in the NRC's premise that a public utility's regulated status in and of itself is sufficient to assure that a utility will have funds sufficient to protect public health and safety. The NRC was ordered to reconsider its decision.

With the appellate court holding the door open, Green, on behalf of a trio of Missouri groups—the Coalition for the Environment, Missourians for Safe Energy, and the Crawdad Alliance—asked the NRC in April 1984 to allow them to challenge UE's pending operating license for the Callaway plant, alleging Union Electric was in shaky financial condition. Three years earlier, the groups' efforts to intervene in the NRC's consideration of the Callaway operating license had been denied. The appellate court action gave them and other groups around the country new hope that challenges to nuclear reactor licenses could be successful.

But in June, the NRC issued a "statement of policy" precluding consideration of financial qualifications in operating-license deliberations.

In July, it rejected Green's effort to re-start the Callaway challenge. And on October 4, 1984, it voted to give UE its full-power operating license. A week later, the new rule eliminating financial considerations in operating license review took effect. The NRC now said that while financial considerations could be considered in applications to construct nuclear plants, no financial consideration was needed in applications for licenses to operate.

In January 1985, Green's clients brought the matter to the attention of the appellate court, as did the New England Coalition on Nuclear Pollution and the other groups whose lawsuit had resulted in the court's remand of the rule back to the NRC. "In its headlong rush to license new nuclear plants before the November [1984] elections," Green told the court, "the commission chose 'to ignore the advice of all its legal advisors and to act as if the 1982 rule were still valid.'" (Green was quoting here from Commissioner James K. Asselstine, in his dissent to the NRC's statement of policy published the previous June.) "Indeed," Green continued, "one of the commissioners [Frederick M. Bernthal] has so little respect for the rule of law that he took the occasion to record his view that it 'is unfortunate that the commission was required to consider elaborate arguments and interpretations based on legal precedent.'" (Green was quoting Bernthal's published views on the same statement of policy.)

"The commission's interpretation of this court's ruling . . . is clearly incorrect. . . . The issuance [to UE] of the low-power operating license and subsequently the full-power operating license while refusing to consider financial qualifications as of the current year was clearly contrary to the effective regulations and in conflict with this court's ruling."

The two appeals were consolidated and the court heard arguments on October 11, 1985. By July 11, 1986, the three-judge panel—Abner Mikva, Ruth Bader Ginsburg, and Robert Bork—had reached their decision. The New England petition was denied, and the Coalition's petition was dismissed.

The Atomic Energy Act, the judges held, "gives the NRC complete discretion to decide what financial qualifications are appropriate." With respect to the Coalition's case, they wrote: "Because of the [NRC's] decision to retain the remanded rule temporarily, petitioners, who in April of 1984 sought for the first time to raise financial qualification issues, were unable to do so. . . . Petitioners argue that [the NRC's denial of their motions] was illegal. Although our previous decision did not expressly vacate the 1982 rule, petitioners claim that once we declared the adoption of the rule irrational, the commission was precluded from applying it, even on an interim basis. We need not reach the merits of this claim. . . . We have now affirmed the commission's new rule, which eliminates case-by-case financial qualifications review for regulated utilities. A remand to the commission so that it could apply this rule and again deny petitioners' motions would be pointless."

CHAPTER 4

A BITTER FIVE-YEAR FIGHT
TO SAVE THE MISSOURI BOTTOMS

Florence Shinkle

THE LARGEST RIVER SYSTEM IN NORTH AMERICA JOINS UP IN THE ST. LOUIS AREA
where the Missouri River converges with the Mississippi. In its endless
gougings and floodings, its givings and takings, this great waterway has
created the richest flood plains in the world, blessed with soils estimated
to dive down 90 feet.

The Missouri River alone, which forms the border between St. Louis
and St. Charles counties, has about 66,000 acres of fertile black soil
composing its "bottoms" in the metro area, 22,000 of those within the
boundaries of St. Louis County. Until 1971, these bottoms were mostly
farmland, a sea of brown striped by the occasional farm road. The area's
agricultural status appeared to be protected by a St. Louis County zoning
ordinance that classified it as "flood plain" and designated it for low-
intensity uses like golf courses, parks, and farming that were compatible
with the river's normal flooding and channel carving.

But that zoning classification created a false sense of security. The
political mindset of successive county administrations, both Republican
and Democratic, was (and is) pro-development and pro-business.
Republican county executives such as Lawrence K. Roos and Eugene
McNary and Democratic leader "Buzz" Westfall shared a vision of the
local manifest destiny as maximizing tax revenues and bricking up St.
Louis County from one end to the other.

Testimony to that monocular vision for the area is the "sales pam-
phlet" prepared by county government employees in 1969 to tout the

benefits of developing the bottoms to elected officials. Written by Ray Patton, director of planning for St. Louis County, and titled "Missouri Bottoms—A Planned Concept for Industry, Commerce and Recreation," it opens: "If the 22,000 acre area along the Missouri River in St. Louis County, known as the Missouri Bottoms, were to be protected by adequate urban type flood protection levees, it could be developed as an intensive industrial, commercial and recreational complex."

The document's diagrams designate the flood plains for research parks, industrial parks, "terraced apartments," barge docking facilities, a bus feeder system. . . . One small island in the southwest area, near Howell Island, is appointed as wildlife habitat.

"At full development, the new land should provide nearly $38,000,000 in new revenue to the four school districts and to the County government," the 1969 pamphlet entices.

Ironically, also in 1969, the U.S. Congress approved the National Environmental Policy Act (NEPA), a groundbreaking effort to address the loss of environmental resources by mandating supervising federal agencies to prepare an environmental impact statement (EIS) for proposed projects that could have significant adverse environmental effects. No permitting action on the part of the agency and no action by proponents of the project could begin until the EIS was completed.

At best, the law gave legal empowerment and encouragement to federal agencies to protect diligently the resources they oversaw. At the very least, the research involved in preparing an environmental impact statement insured that the agency had thoroughly considered the environmental consequences of a project before it was permitted. But of course, environmentalists hoped for the optimum benefit: that NEPA would make ecological warriors out of federal agencies that had been conciliators and consultants.

A MAN WITH A PLAN

IN 1971, DALE PERKINSON, THEN 35, THE PRESIDENT OF LINCLAY DEVELOPMENT Corp., proposed building a 1,600-acre residential and commercial development in the Missouri flood plain, and the St. Louis County Council greeted him as the agent of their fondest ambitions for St. Louis County.

Perkinson, who favored loud checked jackets and bold plans, proposed a $300 million mixed-use development for the flood plain near
Creve Coeur Creek, abutting the city of Bridgeton to the north and east
and bounded by the Missouri River on the west. All the new building
would be protected from river flooding by a two-and-a-half-mile levee
beginning at the Norfolk and Western railroad tracks to the north and
tying into Interstate 70 near St. Charles Rock Road on the south. Sewage
treatment service would come from a wastewater treatment plant already
under consideration by the Metropolitan Sewer District, the local storm-
water and waste disposal authority for the area. Importantly, Perkinson
planned to build the whole shebang using no federal monies, thereby
escaping the oversight that accompanied acceptance of federal funds.

This huge building proposal, one that presaged a mighty change to an
ancient landscape, sailed through both the County Planning and Zoning
Commission and the County Council in less than three months. The
only protests against it came from individual citizens and from Alf Stole,
the mayor of Bridgeton, the St. Louis County municipality that would
bear the impact of increased traffic and loss of open space. Stole hired
Lewis Green as Bridgeton city attorney, with the specific task of contain-
ing Perkinson's development in unincorporated St. Louis County.

Meanwhile, the local office of the Army Corps of Engineers, the
federal agency charged with protecting the nation's navigable waterways,
had no interest in creating waves for Perkinson's flood plain project. Far
from challenging the proposed construction as a potential environmental
threat or preparing a statement of its negative consequences, the Corps
facilitated it, to the extent of providing consultants who advised Linclay
workers on how to expand an existing agricultural levee into an urban
flood protection levee that would meet Corps specifications.

Environmentalists were stunned at the ease with which Perkinson's
cement trucks had breached the natural world along the river.

No one was more disgusted with the Corps' pandering to Linclay
than Lewis Green, who regarded the chumminess between the developer
and the engineers as an egregious circumvention of the Corps' obligations under NEPA.

Green interpreted NEPA to mean that overseeing federal agencies
were supposed to execute their specific duties in a way that *aggressively*

defended environmental interests. So why was the Corps advising Linclay where to dump cement?

And where was the Corps' EIS on the first major building project in the Missouri flood plains, a significant action if ever there was one?

Pushing NEPA

The Corps' response to that second question meant war.

The Corps disclaimed any responsibility for pulling together an impact statement for Earth City, contending it had no legal jurisdiction over the levee it had been helping Linclay construct because the levee was not in an area of the flood plain where the Corps normally had governance. The dike was set too far back from the ordinary high water mark of the Missouri River for the Corps to be accountable for its environmental impact, the Corps spokesman maintained. So the government engineers were being good guys and giving free advice instead.

This evasion seemed particularly nonsensical to Green because the Corps admitted openly that it was advising Linclay to build the levee in a manner that would make it suitable for inclusion in the Pick Sloan levee system, the system running down the Missouri River from Sioux City, Iowa, to St. Louis, over which the Corps *did* have authority under the 1902 Rivers and Harbors Act.

Judicial clarification of the Corps' regulatory jurisdiction and duties became a second intent of the lawsuit filed in 1972 to halt the Linclay development. With Green as the lawyer for the plaintiffs, the Coalition for the Environment, SCENE—a St. Charles–based environmental organization—and three individual co-plaintiffs filed suit in federal district court. (Originally, there were three separate suits against allegedly negligent federal agencies and Linclay. They were later consolidated.)

The plaintiffs asked the court to halt construction of Earth City and the levee that would protect it until the governing federal agencies had performed their duties as environmental stewards responsible to the citizens of the United States "to provide leadership in protecting and enhancing the quality of the Nation's environment to sustain and enrich human life."

The suit asked the court to order the Corps and other federal agencies to meet their obligations under NEPA—to consult with other agencies on the effects of the project and to prepare an environmental impact statement on how such a project in the flood plain might "permanently alter, injure and impair the environmental quality" of the region.

Named as defendants along with the Corps and Linclay were:

• The U.S. Department of Transportation. The DOT had worked out an agreement with Linclay and the Corps that permitted the challenged levee to tie into the embankment of Interstate 70, near St. Charles Rock Road, at a point where the embankment was three feet lower than Corps specifications said was the minimum needed for flood control.

• The Environmental Protection Agency. The EPA, the lawsuit alleged, had not sought public participation as required by the Federal Water Pollution Control Act before it permitted the Metropolitan Sewer District to build a wastewater treatment plant in part to service the Linclay projects. The permit was granted without benefit of public hearings.

The lawsuit had a Mouse-That-Roared quality. A lone lawyer and a couple of conservation groups aimed to halt a multi-million dollar development and get a judicial order compelling federal agencies to assist with their current battle to protect the flood plain and future ones as well.

How much of that agenda did Green realistically hope to accomplish? He was a guy who hid his idealism under intellect and bleak wit. But in certain passages of the lawsuit, you sense the emotion beneath the legal mind: The failure of the supervising agencies to do their respective duties meant that development, Green wrote in the lawsuit, would "destroy fish, cover rich farmland with roads and buildings and fill open spaces with concrete, steel, people, automobiles, trucks, noise, air pollution and waste." In that description pulses an appeal for an endangered world.

"It was the beginning of the environmental movement, and I think Lew believed we had a strong legal case," recalls John Nichols, one of the co-plaintiffs of that 1972 battle. Nichols, a professor at Lindenwood College, was a founder of St. Charles–based SCENE. "In the beginning, we all had hope, but we were up against a tide. And Meredith kept ruling against us again and again."

A GOOD OL' JUDGE

HEARING THE CASE FOR THE MISSOURI EASTERN DISTRICT WAS JUDGE JAMES Meredith from tiny Doniphan, Missouri, near the Arkansas border. Rick Lageson, who worked for the law firm of Green, Hennings and Henry in the 1970s, recalls Meredith as having stuffed animal heads on his chamber's walls, a signal to environmentalists that he probably had the furniture of good ol' boy politics as well. He would be unlikely to favor federal intrusions on local land use and his wilderness protection considerations probably extended only as far as proposals to lengthen the hunting season. He quickly demonstrated his disinclination to reverse St. Louis County's approval of Earth City or restrict any development in the interest of conservation.

Judge Meredith granted the defendants' motion to dismiss on the grounds that the Coalition and the other plaintiffs "lacked standing" to sue, meaning that they had not suffered injury from the development sufficient to entitle them to relief from the court.

What constituted "standing to sue" in environmental battles was still being disputed and defined in the early 1970s, so Judge Meredith's dismissal was not particularly disheartening. Most of the changes broadening the legal interpretation of standing had been gained on appeal, and that path was open to Green.

But Meredith's dismissal order boded ill if Green were to win on appeal and then see the case remanded to Meredith for trial. The wording of Meredith's ruling shows that he just didn't "get it" about what was at stake. What the plaintiffs cast as a precious natural resource Meredith saw as just another piece of open ground that two parties wanted to do different things with. The judge expressed about as much responsibility toward the protection of the eco-region as a lumberman estimating the board feet in a Sequoia: "The only injury to plaintiff is the apparent fact that the actions of defendants are personally displeasing or distasteful

to them due to the parties' differing philosophies of land use planning,"
Meredith wrote. "The plaintiffs want open space, while the corporate defendants want a planned urban community. Judicial preference does not
extend under the Administrative Procedure Act to those who seek to do
no more than vindicate their own value preferences."

Lageson insists Lew Green expected no better from a lower court in
Missouri.

"One of the things we were always aware of was the political orienta-
tion of the judges," Lageson recalled. "They thought all environmentalists
were wacky, publicity-seeking do-gooders. I've never known a trial judge
who was sympathetic to an environmental cause. Almost invariably, the
victories we won were in the court of appeals, somewhat removed from
local political pressure."

A Reversal

Sure enough, when a panel of judges with the 8ᵀᴴ U.S. Circuit Court
of Appeals took up the matter, they reversed Meredith's finding and re-
buked him for his dismissal of the plaintiffs' claims of injury as mere
zoning disagreements.

In *Sierra Club v. Morton*, the U.S. Supreme Court had already decided that individual plaintiffs didn't have to actually use the property
under development to experience injury at the loss of it. Nor did they
have to show economic injury from its development. *Aesthetic loss was
sufficient injury*, the court held.

Traffic jams, loss of the opportunity to view natural scenes—those
adverse effects to broad groups of people not living on a piece of land
with a disputed use also counted as injury, the court had opined. The
historic decision enabled conservation groups to claim a personal stake
in the loss of open space and right to sue in many cases previously off-
limits to them.

No doubt Meredith knew of this historic ruling, occurring as it did
just as he was starting to take up the Linclay Development issues in 1972.
Yet in his own decision to dismiss, he ignored it.

The appellate court delivered a scornful reprimand of the lower
court's failure to take the high court's decision into account: "The

Supreme Court's opinion in *Sierra Club v. Morton* is unequivocal that those who claim only injury of a non-economic nature may also have standing," the opinion read.

"Judge Meredith . . . terms plaintiffs' injuries to be no more than 'personal displeasure.' We disagree with this characterization. As this court views plaintiffs' allegations, they assert injury beyond mere displeasure. Individual plaintiffs . . . claim particularized injury stemming in various ways from the loss of open space and the changes occasioned. . . . Such allegations constitute more than simple assertions of distaste or displeasure. They are statements of specific injury."

So Green opened up the avenue for future environmental groups to challenge projects in the 8th Circuit. An August 1974 article in the *St. Louis Post-Dispatch* termed the appeals ruling "a victory for environmentalists."

A QUALIFIED WIN

BUT IT WAS A LIMITED VICTORY. IN THE THREE YEARS SINCE THE SUIT WAS FILED, the levee and interchange had already been built, and the Coalition knew there would be no unbuilding. Nor had Meredith's attitude toward the issues returned to him for trial altered from the conventional local wisdom that the suit amounted to an attempt to usurp local planning authority via questionable federal legislation.

F. William McAlpin, attorney for Linclay, summarized the view popular in St. Louis County political circles: "The suit is an attempt to overturn the zoning decision of the St. Louis County Council. The environmentalists opposed the zoning. This suit amounts to an end run."

Co-plaintiff John Nichols recalls, "Meredith ruled against us over and over."

Green was determined, however, to make the Corps take responsibility for levee projects in the flood plain. If he could force the Corps to own up to jurisdiction over those systems under NEPA, he could turn the Corps into a weapon, albeit a reluctant one, to arrest future developments in the floodway. Anyway, he hoped he could.

Given the prevailing local outlook and Meredith's demonstrated sympathy toward it, Green probably never could have had a chance to interrogate the Corps on its responsibilities and jurisdiction in open court. But in the end, the Corps agreed it was accountable for levees built far inland of the high water bank of the river where the agency had once claimed its jurisdiction ended.

Why the turnaround?

A PROBING DEPOSITION

IT CAN BE TRACED BACK TO A SEEMINGLY INNOCUOUS DEPOSITION OF THE CORPS' chief permit officer in Kansas City, one Frank Straub. All of Green's patient, solitary, undramatic research that preceded his battles, his mastery of detail and his delight in skewering smug and unsuspecting victims are on display in his interrogation of Straub. Straub had been brought to St. Louis for the deposition, which Green had promised would focus mainly on construction technicalities of the Earth City levee. Engineers *love* to talk about construction technicalities, so Straub happily answered the first question and things went downhill from there.

> *Green: What areas of impact do you consider before you grant a permit for a levee and development?*

> *Straub: We are required to consider the probable effects of the project on navigation, on flood heights and drift, on beach erosion, on fish and wildlife, on pollution and on aesthetics.*

> *Green: Define your area of jurisdiction, please.*

> *Straub: The Corps assumes jurisdiction for permitting projects up to or just below the high bank of its rivers.*

> *Green: You used the term "high bank." Can you tell me what that means to you?*

> *Straub: High bank is defined as that point where the vegetation changes from marine type to land type.*

> *Green: If it's a close question as to whether some vegetation was marine type or land type, there are experts to whom it could be referred?*

Straub: Yessir.

Green: You don't refer every application (for permit) to your vegetation expert, do you?

Straub: Nossir.

Green: What portion do you decide yourself?

Straub: Oh, 95 percent. Only in those areas where it's questionable do we consider sending an expert down to investigate the site.

Green: Can you give me some examples of marine type vegetation?

Straub: I don't believe I'm qualified to answer that question [even though he feels qualified to determine the necessity for permits in 95 percent of all cases based on whether a project is in an area with land or marine vegetation.]

Green: Can you give me some examples of land type vegetation?

Straub: I don't believe I'm qualified to answer that. My rule of thumb is: if it's close, I notify the person that the permit is required.

Green then produced a 1938 permit, with accompanying drawings, issued by the Corps to the Kaw Valley Drainage District of Wyandotte County, Kansas, "to repair and reconstruct a revetment."

Green: Can you tell me, looking at the drawing, where the work for which a permit was issued is located with respect to the high bank of the water?

Straub: Whoever prepared this drawing, they show a bank line of the river, and this revetment work is several hundred feet landward of this point.

Green: So in some places that levee might be as much as a thousand feet or more from what you call the bank of the river?

Straub: The district noted that bank.

Green: Can you tell me what type of vegetation exists in the vicinity of the work?

Straub: Nossir.

Further questions center on circumstances surrounding a 1960 construction project undertaken by the Corps on the Missouri River.

Green: This levee is landward of the high water mark?

Straub: Yessir.

Green: So the Corps itself sometimes builds levees above the standard high water mark?

Straub: Yessir. . . . Yes, we do build levees above the standard high water bank.

With the agency's definition of its jurisdictional area ripped to shreds and with enough ammunition at the ready to detonate a firestorm of bad publicity for the Corps if the contents of the deposition should be aired in court, the agency agreed to rethink where it was accountable for construction oversight.

In June 1976, the Coalition for the Environment, SCENE, and lead attorney Green formally gave up the fight to dismantle Earth City in exchange for two major concessions: the award of a 123-acre corridor running along the river side of the Earth City levee and an agreement by the Corps to take jurisdiction of the Missouri flood plain, not just to the high bank of the river itself but to the high water bank of all tributaries joining it.

Green was pleased. A *Post-Dispatch* article by Marjorie Mandel quotes the attorney calling the settlement with the Corps "a major victory" and "a very valuable tool in preserving flood plains everywhere."

In the Coalition's own newsletter, Green is quoted: "The settlement recognizes that the levee, if it were built today, would require a Corps permit, and it is our belief that this new rule will similarly require the Corps to assert jurisdiction over major encroachments on the flood plains of the major rivers of the continent."

So the bitter five-year war ended in a season of hopefulness. Next time a big building project loomed for the flood plains, the mighty regulatory agency overseeing the waterways would have to behave as an agent of conservation, Green believed. If there were another court challenge, perhaps they would draw a sympathetic judge, one less reflective of local interests than Meredith proved to be.

But, ominously, the first flood plain building had gone forward. At the close of legal hostilities, although Dale Perkinson himself had gone broke and a new developer had stepped in, Earth City had 23 buildings and the waste water treatment plant and highway exchange that the plaintiffs had tried to stop.

A precedent had been set.

CHAPTER 5

A PLAN FOR A SPORTS DOME
IS FOILED, BUT WETLANDS
ARE STILL LOST

Florence Shinkle

THE FEARFUL RUMORS BEGAN IN LATE 1984.

"CARDINALS CHANGING THEIR ROOST?" the *St. Louis Post-Dispatch* queried worriedly.

Other cities were courting the city's major-league football team, making mating noises to Cardinals owner Bill Bidwill, promising lavish stadiums and increased profits for the team if it would transplant itself to their cities. Baltimore, Jacksonville, even New York were all reported as suitors.

Bidwill, who had bought out his brother Stormy in 1976 to become the team's sole owner, protested that he wanted to keep the team here but-t-t. . . .

He needed a 70,000-seat stadium. A domed, all-weather one. Never mind that the Cards, who then played in Busch Stadium, rarely filled its 51,000 seats. Bidwill wanted a giant $150 million, all-weather home for his team. Or else.

And so began the panicked storm of wheeling and dealing that in turn led to a proposal to build a giant football stadium in the flood plains of the Missouri Bottoms in an area called Riverport.

"Keep the birds in their nest," the Missouri Quarterback Club pleaded, seeking public support for the idea.

"Keep St. Louis a Big League City," pleaded a handout from UNICOM, the public relations firm hired by St. Louis County Supervisor Eugene McNary to hype the proposal.

Of all the dumb ideas, this one had to rank as the dumbest, not just because of the disastrous environmental impact of the massive weekly treks into a fragile ecosystem, but also because of the financial damage to the equally fragile economy of downtown St. Louis from the loss of game-goers' revenues.

Yet the frantic, hyperactive rush to prevent the team's threatened departure swept logic and judgment aside. Political honchos, labor leaders, community figures, and crowds of football lovers joined league in the battle to "keep 'em home in the Dome," as one aerial banner in support of the Riverport project advertised.

It was a little like being the sole soldier dropped behind enemy lines to oppose this crush, but the Coalition for the Environment determined it would take a stand against its old adversary, the U.S. Army Corps of Engineers. To the Coalition and attorney Lewis Green, it was obvious that the regulatory agency charged with protecting the wetlands was playing ball with the stadium builders just as it had a decade earlier with the developers of Earth City.

Fronting for the County

Exactly how much the Corps knew about the plan for a stadium in Riverport before it approved the development's levee is unclear. Certainly, conservation groups felt the entire permitting process had been manipulated to serve the interests of the engineering firm Sverdrup Corp. and St. Louis County, with the plan for the stadium being hidden by all parties until the permit was approved.

Riverport, the area proposed for the stadium location, began as a planned 550-acre commercial and industrial center south of and adjacent to Interstate 70 across from Earth City. In October 1983, St. Louis–based Sverdrup, one of the nation's largest engineering firms, requested a permit from the Corps to construct a 500-year levee to protect the acreage under development.

Sverdrup's original plans for the levee included construction of an outfall arm that would have shunted surface water pollutants from the development out onto the riverbanks. Instead of nixing the whole plan because of the ill-conceived design for putting contaminants in the river, the Corps helped Sverdrup alter the plan to delete the outfall and replace it with a retention basin. Then the Corps announced that, as a result of the modifications, no permit for the construction would be required under the Rivers and Harbors Act of 1899, which regulates discharges into the nation's streams. All that would be needed was a second permit for filling the wetlands for the levee construction itself, a permit for which many previous applications had been granted. To conservationists, it looked like the Corps, from the start of its dealings with Sverdrup, was setting up the corporation for success.

In October 1984, the Corps began the public hearing process for a permit for levee construction. The date for the beginning of the Corps' review coincided with the period when rumors intensified about the Cardinals needing a new stadium or else. But at the Corps' public hearings for Riverport, Sverdrup presented designs for a mundane stadium-free development, typical of what, sadly, had been going into the flood plain in the 15 years since St. Louis County first devised its design for the bottoms. As the Coalition's subsequent lawsuit against Riverport and the stadium conceded poignantly, Sverdrup's initial development seemed the sort that "notwithstanding the opposition of plaintiff Coalition, . . . has moved steadily forward" in the flood plain.

As the review process continued, press reports mounted about the possibility of St. Louis County spearheading construction of a stadium in Riverport. The Corps leaders denied any knowledge of this. To prove they were innocent of knowledge of any such scheme, they produced communications between the agency and Sverdrup in which the Corps dutifully inquired about the possibility of a stadium in Riverport—and received assurances that no such plan was in the offing: "On or about March 29, 1985, the Sverdrup defendants responded by letter that *the Sverdrup defendants* had no plans to construct a stadium in Riverport," the Corps said. Which was accurate as far as it went, since St. Louis County was the entity planning to build the stadium.

In May 1985, the Corps issued Sverdrup a permit authorizing levee construction and discharge of fill into surrounding wetlands for the commercial and industrial Riverport development. Less than two weeks later, Sverdrup began or resumed discussions with St. Louis County about the County buying land in Riverport for a stadium. And by mid-June, Sverdrup had given McNary a draft sale contract for the purchase of land at Riverport. Negotiations over the sale of the land continued for the next five months.

On November 12, 1985, the Corps formally got word about plans for a stadium in Riverport on 100 acres purchased from Riverport by St. Louis County. There's no record of who at the Corps' St. Louis offices acted totally flabbergasted and astounded at the news. Two days later the press carried the story along with a report that parking lots would be built in the wetlands.

A REVOLVING DOOR

MEANWHILE, MCNARY HAD SHREWDLY HIRED ONE OF THE CORPS' OWN TO DEAL with the Corps on permitting issues. Working as a consultant for St. Louis County was Leon McKinney, a former colonel with the Corps and lead officer in the agency's St. Louis office before his retirement. The chumminess between him and the permitting officers was covert and exclusive. From the Coalition's lawsuit: "Thereafter, the Corps and Sverdrup had many communications between one another . . . to discuss the plan (for a stadium). The Corps defendants repeatedly admitted representatives of the St. Louis County government to those meetings, but steadfastly excluded the public."

Other aspects of the McNary campaign to build a stadium in Riverport demonstrated equal foresight and calculation:

To finance the land purchase, McNary got the St. Louis County Council to authorize the use of $1 million from the county's convention and tourism fund, which he declared was no longer needed for tourism. To construct the levee for the stadium, he drew on $3 million from the transportation trust fund, a mass-transit and road improvement fund.

As for the cost of building the stadium itself, McNary's idea was to issue revenue bonds, to be paid off out of the proceeds from rents and ticket sales.

"Not one penny of taxpayer money will be used in the construction," McNary promised in a film made to garner public support. "Join us in our vision . . . in our bold step toward the 21st century. Help us build our Dome, a magnet for future growth."

Meanwhile, he courted Bill Bidwill for a commitment to bring his team to the Dome, a move that infuriated St. Louis Mayor Vincent Schoemehl, who was turning over rocks looking for ways and means to keep the team downtown.

To try to provide for Bidwill's team, the city fathers proposed building a multi-purpose center alongside the downtown Convention Center. But Mayor Schoemehl's own polls showed the tax increase necessary to fund such an undertaking would never get voter approval. For plan B Schoemehl proposed a smaller expansion of the Convention Center. He was successful in pushing that building plan with the Board of Aldermen, but it was inadequate as a new home for the Cardinals.

None of this flailing about was lost on Bill Bidwill. He was behaving more and more like a team owner who was about to break his lease. He announced he would only continue to play in Busch Stadium if the place no longer sold Budweiser beer, a condition on a par with forbidding China to serve rice.

In April 1986, Bidwill gave McNary a semi-commitment, taking an option to buy the 100 acres the county had bought for the stadium, plus another option on an additional 300 acres. He told McNary that he would move his team to the would-be Riverport dome if construction got underway before the end of 1987.

The publicity campaign around this coup included a dismissive note about the opposition, "Right now the dome project is being threatened by a small but vocal group. . . ."

A Battle on Three Fronts

Lewis Green and the Coalition for the Environment filed suit in federal district court in June 1986, seeking to set aside the permit for Riverport and halt construction of the stadium.

At the same time, attorney Peter Schmitz, acting as lead attorney for the Open Space Council and the League of Women Voters, Missouri chapter, challenged in Circuit Court McNary's use of the taxpayer-financed tourism and transportation trust funds to purchase land and build improvements for the stadium.

Mayor Schoemehl and Thomas "Red" Villa, the bald, tough, charming southsider who headed up the St. Louis Board of Aldermen, started playing a little undercover hardball themselves, approaching city developers, do-gooders, and the heads of downtown corporations seeking donations to help fund the Coalition's suit. So much for the ballyhooed city-county cooperation.

As soon as the federal suit was filed, the Corps went into defensive mode, announcing that it would re-evaluate its own decision to allow the stadium to be constructed without a new permitting study or an environmental impact statement. The claim to re-evaluate was a shrewd legal gambit because it made the Coalition's lawsuit seem premature, a request for redress of an action not yet finalized. Sure enough, the court dismissed all claims against the stadium and its improvements, saying they were not "ripe for review."

Green then settled the first suit via a consent degree that allowed all Riverport construction except the stadium, which the Coalition reserved the right to sue over again.

In return for giving up its case against all of Riverport, the plaintiffs received $100,000 and the guarantee of an environmental impact statement being completed if the northerly, still-undeveloped section of the Creve Coeur bottoms became a development target. It would not be the last time that Green used the terms of one court settlement to position himself for the next battle. And the hundred grand came in handy to help the Coalition pay legal expenses.

"All the parties in the suit won. We all came away with something," Green was quoted as telling the *Post-Dispatch* in a March 1987 article.

A Sham Review

But what Green seemed to be unable to win through the courts or negotiations was the cooperation of the Corps in the protection of the bottoms.

The Corps' re-evaluation of the permit, completed after the original lawsuit was dismissed, seemed to Green and other conservationists a disingenuous sham.

"This entire process of re-evaluation was conducted without publication of notice, without affording the public an opportunity to be heard and without engaging in the consultation with interested state and federal authorities required by applicable statutes and regulations," the Coalition charged in the lawsuit it refiled after the Corps' predictable decision was announced.

Following its "re-evaluation," the Corps had found: "The construction of a domed stadium and some parking facilities on 100 acres of the Riverport site previously planned for commercial, retail and industrial use of a non-specific nature does not increase the scope of the permitted activity.

"Since there will be no additional placement of fill in the wetlands resulting from the construction of the revised project, there is no significant increase in the scope of the activity that would require the processing of a new application for a permit."

So, since the amount of mud excavated and filled remained the same, the impact of stadium activity on the bottoms was not a matter for which the Corps had legal responsibility.

The Corps also concluded it would not require a permit for parking areas around the stadium because there would be a 50-foot buffer between the asphalted areas and the wetlands that the Corps was supposed to protect. The Corps therefore had "no jurisdiction," it declared, and development of the parking lots could proceed without agency approval.

The outcry at that evasion of duty wasn't just from the Coalition. Joe Tieger, on staff with the U.S. Fish and Wildlife Service, an agency that holds a consulting role with the Corps, blasted his fellow federal employees: "As expected the Corps has taken the narrowest possible view of their responsibilities," Tieger is quoted in a *Post-Dispatch* article.

Roger Pryor, program director for the Coalition, snapped, "Once again the Corps is sidestepping its responsibility to regulate the wetlands in that area and for that matter the flood plain."

Back in Court

Green filed his second suit, in July 1987, probably expecting defeat in the judicial arena but victory in the race against the clock. A month earlier, the Corps had issued its decision not to require a new, separate permit for stadium construction, and after the much publicized, 16-month re-assessment, Green could not have harbored much hope that the court would order the Corps to perform an EIS as well. However, Bidwill had given the county an end-of-the-year deadline for construction to begin on a new stadium for him even to consider keeping the Cardinals in St. Louis. So another six months of funding and building proposals being tied up in county and federal court would open the door for the team's departure. The wisdom of paying for a Dome with no home team to play in it would be one for investors to decide.

Moreover, Green had powerful allies. Both the city of St. Louis and the League of Women Voters became plaintiffs and openly contributed to the legal fund. The League sent a representative to serve on the No-Dome Committee, organized to counter McNary's Dome Committee. Mayor Schoemehl assigned city attorneys to help Green and to co-sign Green's new petition to the court seeking to stop the stadium until the Corps undertook an EIS.

McNary was furious: "Here I was trying to build a stadium and the city filed suit to stop me," he recalled later in a *Post-Dispatch* article published January 17, 1988. "The establishment actually paid for the environmentalists to file suit."

Seeing the depth of the divide, Bidwill began traveling to various cities to listen to their offers, playing high-stakes poker and holding all the good cards.

Predictably, the Coalition's second lawsuit failed both at the trial and appeals levels.

At the trial level, after a five-day bench trial, the judge found for the defendants, the Army Corps, on all claims.

Reviewing the record, the court found that the Corps had solicited evidence and testimony from every party it was supposed to and consumed 16 months in the process. This, the court said, constituted a comprehensive evaluation.

Green had not shown to the court's satisfaction that any relevant information had been omitted. And the court could only rule on whether the study had been sufficient, not on whether the Corps made the "right" decision upon review:

"Opponents failed to show that the Army Corps of Engineers had omitted from the administrative record facts which would require an environmental impact statement with respect to construction of the domed football stadium on land where the permit to fill the wetlands already had been issued.

"The decision not to modify or revoke the permit issued by the Army Corps of Engineers for discharge of fill material into the wetland area *is one committed to the Corps' absolute discretion.*"

The court also agreed with the Corps that the agency's permitting authority extended only to the building of the levee and the filling of the wetlands with dredge material and did not extend to the nature of the structure eventually built on the fill. "The activity permitted by the Corps is not the construction of an industrial park or a stadium; it is the filling of wetlands necessary to construction an 800-foot levee," the court ruled. "The substitution of a stadium for some unspecified industrial facility does not change the scope of that activity."

The appeals court later upheld the decision. So the Corps was granted a back-door escape route from having to take responsibility for what was built in the flood plain. All it had to do was follow its own rules for reviewing an application and count how many tons of fill were going into the flood plain. It need never worry about the environmental impact of the specific development proposed.

The Open Space Council's suit in Circuit Court met a similar fate: All claims were dismissed as to whether McNary had misused funds from the transportation and tourism trust funds when he bought the land and improvements for the Dome.

Off to Phoenix

But by this time—the end of 1987—Bidwill had decided to move. He would end up in Phoenix with his team, where businessmen swore they'd build him a dome and where meanwhile the team would play in Arizona State University's Sun Devil Stadium, which was expanded to 73,000 seats to meet Bidwill's demands.

After the Circuit Court upheld the county's right to buy the 100 acres for the now-scrapped stadium using tourism fund dollars, McNary continued to try to spin other stadium deals. He finally abandoned the effort as plans for a downtown dome took shape. The county leased the land for soybeans until it was resold, at a profit, to private interests for development. According to Jim Lahey, McNary's advisor, developers fought over the tract, figuring their plans were bound to get Corps approval "since nothing they could dream up would match building a stadium for intensive land use."

No dome has ever been built in the bottoms.

So, in one sense, the Coalition's fight against a stadium in Riverport could be termed a victory. But underneath the applause runs a minor-key threnody of loss. The battle made clear not only that the Corps would never independently ally itself with conservation interests, but also that the courts would never compel the agency to, at least not in Missouri.

For any sympathetic researcher, one of the poignant things about delving through Green's files is the change in tone in his quotes as the long war continued.

After the 1976 Earth City settlement when the Corps accepted responsibility for jurisdiction of the flood plains as well as the rivers, the tone was one of near-exultation.

From a June 1976 *Post-Dispatch* article: "Green called the (Earth City) settlement 'a very major victory' and predicted that the ruling expanding the Corps jurisdiction over the flood plain would be 'a very, very valuable tool in helping to preserve flood plains everywhere.'"

Years later, Green commented: "There aren't many laws that will help me. Demanding an environmental impact statement is the best I can do. And I never get it. If I did get it, it wouldn't accomplish much except maybe educate the public."

The limits of using NEPA to invoke Corps protection of the flood plains were painfully delineated in the Riverport battles. The first thinking of environmentalists after Congress approved NEPA in 1969 was that the regulatory agencies and the judiciary could be harnessed and used to curb the march of big business across the open spaces. The sad subsequent discovery was that government agencies were no more immune to political pressure than any other interest group. Time and again the Corps worked hard, not at protecting the environment, but at currying goodwill with the powers-that-be whose influence might in turn affect their budget. Industrial development? Permit granted. Sewage treatment plant? Sure. Stadium for 72,000? No difference between it and other entertainment venues.

Nor was there any bold judge out there who had any intention of zoning from the bench and excluding all flood plain uses not in harmony with the environment.

Yet to this day, the strategic wars to mitigate the impact of development in the flood plain continue under the Great Rivers Floodplain Protection Program. The program, established by the Great Rivers Environmental Law Center, the firm established by Green in 2002 to conduct public interest environmental litigation, brings legal challenges against environmentally detrimental flood plain development in the Missouri and Mississippi river bottoms. They are strategic suits, designed to curb the most flagrant abuses. The flood plains are largely covered with concrete and asphalt now, despite the great efforts by Green, the Coalition, and other conservationists to educate the public to the terrible loss it was permitting and furthering.

"We've tried to find some way to do something," Green said in 1993, in a comment that conveys an admission of how frequently he was stymied.

"It is very frustrating, but the alternative is not even trying," he told *Post-Dispatch* reporter Sara Shipley in 2002. "The environment can't fight for itself. Somebody has got to fight for it."

I RECOMMEND!

MADEIRA WILLIAMS

and

LEWIS C. GREEN

for re-election as Democratic Committeewoman and Committeeman of Bonhomme Township.

Since their election in 1958, these two candidates have shown the character and ability required to provide strong party leadership, and to give us the opportunity to vote for the best available candidates for the various elective offices. VOTE for them at the primary election, on Tuesday, August 2, 1960.

Sincerely yours,

MADEIRA WILLIAMS
DEMOCRATIC COMMITTEEWOMAN
BONHOMME TOWNSHIP

LEWIS C. GREEN
DEMOCRATIC COMMITTEEMAN
BONHOMME TOWNSHIP

GO WITH GREEN FOR -

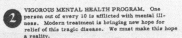

LEWIS C. GREEN

* Married 4 children
* Veteran, World War II
* Lifetime County Resident
* Practicing attorney
* Member: American, Missouri, St. Louis Bar Associations.
* Harvard Law School, magna cum laude
* Law Clerk to Mr. Justice Reed, U.S. Supreme Court, 1951
* Attorney for National Labor Relations Board 1952-54
* Former Lecturer in Legislation, St. Louis University law School
* Former Lecturer in Constitutional Law, Washington University Law School
* Democratic Committeeman, Bonhomme Township, since 1958

1 4-YEAR BRANCH OF MISSOURI UNIVERSITY IN THE METROPOLITAN AREA. Missouri's greatest natural resource is her young people. They must have a chance for higher education that is within their reach, both financially and geographically.

2 VIGOROUS MENTAL HEALTH PROGRAM. One person out of every 10 is afflicted with mental illness. Modern treatment is bringing new hope for relief of this tragic disease. We must make this hope a reality.

3 RIGHT TO VOTE ON NON-PARTISAN COURT PLAN in St. Louis County. Our citizens must no longer be denied the right, guaranteed in the Missouri constitution, to remove politics from the courts.

4 DYNAMIC ST. LOUIS COUNTY GOVERNMENT. Urban growth has created vast problems which cannot be solved by the antiquated machinery provided for the government of St. Louis County. The County and its municipalities must be given the powers needed to solve these modern problems. Orderly growth and a solid tax base can result only from a dynamic county government.

5 EQUAL RIGHTS AND OPPORTUNITIES FOR ALL CITIZENS. Article 1 of the Missouri constitution states: "...all persons are created equal and are entitled to equal rights and opportunities under the law." The legislature must meet its responsibility to give practical meaning to this constitutional guarantee.

6 MORE INDUSTRY AND RECREATION for state and county. Missouri has the climate, water, other natural resources, and labor to become a prosperous state, and a state with fine recreational facilities. Energetic efforts to attract new industry, and prompt development of the Meramec Basin, are vitally needed, for the benefit of the entire state, and especially for the metropolitan area.

7 CONFLICT-OF-INTEREST LEGISLATION. Increased confidence in our government can come about only through the guarantee of fair and impartial administration of laws. Such legislation is long overdue.

****

Vote For

Lewis C. Green

Democrat for State Representative,
11th District, St. Louis County

Tuesday, Nov. 6

1962

GO WITH GREEN

WHAT IS GOING ON AT THE GRASS ROOTS?

A REPORT BY

LEWIS C. GREEN
Democratic
Committeeman

WILMA HORSFALL
Democratic
Committeewoman

BONHOMME TOWNSHIP

Lewis Green as Committeeman Campaign Literature, 1960s

Lewis Green as Democratic Committeeman Meets President Johnson

St. Louis Environmentalists Roger Pryor, Leo Drey, and Lewis Green

Lewis Green at His Desk

Lewis Green at Home

*with his dogs: the lap puppy (above)
grew bigger (right)*

with his wife, Louise

Lewis Green in 2001 when he started Great Rivers Environmental Law Center

Lewis Green designed the logo of Great Rivers Environmental Law Center to reflect St. Louis's location near the confluence of the Illinois, Missouri and Mississippi Rivers.

Great Rivers Environmental Law Center staff: Dorothy Roberson (second from left), office manager, and staff attorneys Bruce Morrison, Kathleen Green Henry, and Henry Robertson.

CHAPTER 6

A SHELL GAME WITH PLUTONIUM, AND A LONG-ODDS BATTLE WITH THE DOE

Patricia Tummons

LEWIS GREEN MAY NOT HAVE WON EVERY LEGAL BATTLE HE TOOK ON, BUT HE fought each one with everything he had. That was one of the things that most impressed Dan Hirsch, director of the California-based Committee to Bridge the Gap, during the years that Green represented his group in a lawsuit against the Department of Energy.

"He was a magnificent human being, incredibly energetic and very bright," Hirsch said, whose group focuses on issues of nuclear safety, waste disposal, proliferation, and disarmament. "He had great kindness and humor. He was basically an incredible environmental warrior."

The lawsuit that Green undertook on behalf of Hirsch and others was a David-and-Goliath pairing. In one corner stood Green and a California-based attorney whose role was little more than to provide the legal wedge that Green needed to practice law in California. Jammed into the opposing one were the seemingly endless ranks of attorneys from the Department of Justice and Department of Energy.

The stakes could not have been higher. At the center of the case was a Department of Energy plan to turn dross (high-level nuclear waste) into something more valuable than gold (weapons- or utility-grade nuclear fuel, with leftover radioactive wastes that could be disposed of on the cheap).

By the time the case wound to a close some seven years after it began, it had morphed into a monster, everything-but-the-kitchen-sink legal pudding that revealed Green's legal wit at its sharpest. Although the litigation ended in a draw, through the court Green and his clients were able to learn the full scope of the Department of Energy's ultimately failed project to develop new ways of reprocessing waste.

The outcome fell short of giving Hirsch and other plaintiffs everything they had sought. However, "it did have a salutary effect," said Hirsch.

"POSSIBLE PROBLEMS FROM AN ACTIVIST GROUP"

THE EVENTS THAT RESULTED IN LEW GREEN FIGHTING A LONELY, LONG-ODDS BATTLE nearly two thousand miles from his home base began in 1989. Rockwell International, a defense contractor, had obtained a contract from several Japanese firms to conduct research into how high-level nuclear waste might be stripped of its more dangerous components. If this could be accomplished, proponents argued, one of the impediments to nuclear energy—the vast volumes of high-level radioactive waste it generated—could be mitigated, clearing the way for additional construction of nuclear power plants.

Rockwell had planned to carry out the research at its Santa Susana Field Laboratory near Los Angeles. But opposition to the project, from nearby residents as well as environmental groups and Hirsch's organization, led to a change in plans. The groups had pressed the Nuclear Regulatory Commission to require an environmental impact statement for the project that would disclose the range of potential hazards associated with it. The Japanese firms, Rockwell, and DOE all objected.

Rockwell then came up with what it thought would be a simple solution to the controversy: Move it to Missouri. Quiet approaches to state officials, administrators with the University of Missouri, and the Columbia, Mo., Chamber of Commerce indicated the project would be received with open arms. By early 1990, Rockwell had sealed the deal, with the university agreeing to let its 10-megawatt research reactor be used to carry out the project known as TRUMP-S (TRansUranic Management by Pyro-partitioning Separation). In return, as a subcontractor, the university would receive several million dollars when the work was done.

Keenly aware of the sensitivity and potential hazards of the project, Rockwell, the NRC, and Mizzou officials conspired to keep it below the radar of the public. In a February 1990 memo, university information officer Marty Oetting cautioned administrators to hold off issuing any news release or other information about the project until after the NRC had issued a license and other agreements were in place, "due to possible problems from an activist group"—Hirsch's—"in California that is instrumental in forcing the research out of that state."

"It is important," Oetting continued, "that the news of this partnership not be released prior to the press conference so we can secure positive media coverage."

Over the next two months, the NRC quietly amended the license of the Mizzou reactor, the largest university research reactor in the country, so as to allow it to undertake the project. In two amendments, it gave the university permission to possess and use in unsealed form 10 grams of plutonium 239/240, 500 grams of depleted uranium, up to 14 grams of neptunium-237, and 7 grams of americium-241.

In April 1990, as the university took possession of the uranium and plutonium needed to start the research, it finally issued a press release announcing the project. By then, everything needed to move the project forward was in place: a special lab had been built, equipment had arrived, and the NRC license amendments for the University of Missouri Research Reactor—or MURR—were in place.

On May 7, the Missouri Coalition for the Environment, the Mid-Missouri Nuclear Weapons Freeze, Inc., and the Physicians for Social Responsibility/Mid-Missouri Chapter, all represented by Lewis Green, were petitioning the NRC's Atomic Safety and Licensing Board for a hearing on the license amendments. The petition noted that before the most recent license amendments, MURR was authorized to possess no more than 5 millicuries of neptunium and 40 millicuries of americium in unsealed form. The NRC license amendments of March to authorize possession of 710 millicuries of plutonium 239 and 240, 10 millicuries of neptunium-237, and 25 curies of americium-241, all in unsealed form, represented a quantum leap in the potential dangers to the environment, but no public notice of the changes was ever given nor had the NRC issued any finding of no significant impact, Green argued.

Initially, the Atomic Safety and Licensing Board's administrative judge, Peter Bloch, seemed sympathetic to the arguments made by Green. In June, he determined that the hearing file that he had ordered the NRC to provide was incomplete and that NRC staff had excluded relevant documents. The NRC staff then put the file together, but not in the fashion the judge had requested. Moreover, it was available only in the NRC reading room in Washington, D.C. In response to the foot-dragging, at the end of July 1990, Bloch issued yet another order, but he seemed helpless to force compliance.

In August, Green finally received from the NRC what he described as a "hearing pile"—an "unindexed, unnumbered, uncitable pile of random documents." Bloch agreed, saying it had "required extensive work by my office to put these documents into an orderly form." On the other hand, he said, "There is no apparent remedy for these irritating circumstances. . . . All I can do is to exhort the staff to be more cooperative in the future."

On October 29, 1990, Bloch finally ordered a temporary stay to the experiments, having found that the groups filing the petition were likely to prevail on a variety of allegations. Mizzou, he said, had failed to show it had complied with requirements for emergency planning, had failed to fully document the radionuclides being worked with, had not shown that its filters were adequate, and had not demonstrated it had competent personnel to work with the materials, among other things.

But by November 16, Bloch reversed himself, lifting the stay and finding that the university's response to his concerns was credible. And, when Bloch issued his final decision in July 1991, he concluded that the safety of the experiments "should not be measured by the extreme scenarios that may be hypothesized." While "greater care is called for in describing plutonium materials than was shown in this application," he wrote, the issue was now moot, since the first phase of the project begun in June 1990 had been completed.

HEDGING BETS

OVER THE YEAR IN WHICH THE CASE WAS BEFORE HIM, JUDGE BLOCH AGONIZED AT length over the TRUMP-S experiments at Mizzou. His discussions of the issues at hand, his vacillations, his opinions that seemed to change with the wind are all set forth *ad nauseam* in the prolix decisions he issued. But the project's opponents, represented by Green, did not place all their bets on the chance that they might prevail before Bloch and, beyond that, the Nuclear Regulatory Commission. Instead, on August 29, 1990, they filed a petition in the U.S. District Court for the Northern District of California.

Plaintiffs were Energy and Resource Advocates, a non-profit organization based in Arcata, California, the Physicians for Social Responsibility/ San Francisco Bay Area Chapter, the Northern California SANE/FREEZE, the Committee to Bridge the Gap, the Southern California Federation of Scientists, the Los Angeles Physicians for Social Responsibility, and Mid-Missouri Nuclear Weapons Freeze, Inc.

Named as defendants were James Watkins, then secretary of Energy; Kenneth Quitoriano, the TRUMP-S project manager in the San Francisco office of the Department of Energy; Donald Pearman, Jr., acting manager of the DOE's San Francisco office; and the Department of Energy itself.

Proponents of the technology that would be advanced if the TRUMP-S project were successful asserted that the technology "has worldwide implications, especially in nuclear nations without land suitable for a high-level waste repository," the complaint noted. On the other hand, in the view of the plaintiffs, the program, "if successful, would in fact increase the volume of highly radioactive waste to be disposed of, thus increasing the difficulties of disposing of those materials safely, that the waste would retain approximately 98 percent of its radioactivity, and that the planned disposal of these high-level radioactive wastes above ground, in low-level waste repositories, would have serious adverse environmental consequences for mankind."

One of the issues raised by the plaintiffs concerned the DOE's failure to prepare an environmental impact statement for the project and the secrecy that surrounded their claimed compliance with the National Environmental Policy Act (NEPA). Although the agency had prepared an environmental assessment for the Missouri project in early 1990, DOE officials had not made it public. As Green wrote in the complaint, "Despite their litigation before the NRC respecting the need for a [National Environmental Policy Act] review, and their inquiries to the

DOE . . . over a period of at least 10 months, none of the plaintiffs was given notice of the existence of any NEPA review process until after the review was completed and a final determination was made not to prepare an EIS."

Not only did the DOE fail to disclose the existence of the environmental assessment, Quitoriano had out-and-out lied to keep the plaintiffs from learning of it. "On April 3 [1990], plaintiff's agent phoned Quitoriano asking whether any NEPA review was in process or was contemplated. Quitoriano refused to acknowledge the existence or disclose the status of any such NEPA review," the complaint stated.

By April 1991, the presiding judge ordered the DOE to produce a list of documents, but otherwise prevented discovery and the taking of depositions. A year later, the DOE had still not provided all the documents to the plaintiffs, prompting Green to seek the court's leave to amend the original complaint. Among other things, he alleged that the defendants concealed not only from the plaintiffs, but also from the NRC, the Environmental Protection Agency, the Department of Defense, the Arms Control and Disarmament Agency, and the Bureau of Land Management "the fact that the defendants were engaged in a NEPA process" and also that they had "avoided soliciting information from those agencies or the public."

In addition, based on new information, the complaint asked the court to expand the list of sites to be included in any DOE analysis of the environmental impacts of the TRUMP-S program. Thanks to the trickle of documents released by the DOE, the true dimensions of the program were revealed to be much broader than the plaintiffs had originally suspected.

Green asked the judge for an injunction staying any further work on the TRUMP-S project, which, he noted, "is still, in 1992, being carried on in violation of generally accepted local, national, and international fire safety standards."

The DOE vigorously opposed the motion to revise the complaint. In addition, it challenged the plaintiffs' standing, saying they had not shown they lived near the sites mentioned in the complaint.

An Encouraging Order

THE BACK-AND-FORTH BETWEEN THE PLAINTIFFS AND THE DOE CONTINUED another four years, with the DOE grudgingly providing documents, usually under order of the judge, and balking at any attempts by the plaintiffs to revise the complaint in light of the new information.

As Green discovered, the DOE had secretly engaged the Massachusetts Institute of Technology to develop an environmental impact statement for the entire TRUMP-S project and, more generally, for the DOE's efforts to develop a new technology to reprocess irradiated nuclear fuel through "pyroprocessing" or "pyropartitioning." This involved placing the waste into a molten salt, heating it to high temperatures, and subjecting it to electric currents. The process was supposed to separate out uranium, plutonium, and other long-lived, highly radioactive elements, or actinides, for re-use as fuel in nuclear reactors.

"In the course of the litigation," Green wrote, "plaintiffs learned that DOE is conducting or sponsoring many other connected projects, at numerous labs in various parts of the country, in an effort to separate actinides from spent nuclear fuel. It became clear to plaintiffs that DOE is conducting or sponsoring a concerted group of such partitioning and transmutation (PT) projects as part of a program to develop a new, more efficient technology." Thus, Green asked the court in 1994 for leave to file a second amended complaint, which argued that all the various PT projects "constitute connected actions, cumulative actions, or similar actions, and that the cumulative impacts of all these actions must be assessed in a single EIS." Green also alleged the DOE was withholding information that, under the Freedom of Information Act, it had no right to withhold.

The DOE asked the court to dismiss claims alleging violations of NEPA, FOIA, and the Nuclear Non-Proliferation Act. In August 1995, Judge Claudia Wilken threw out the DOE's motion for dismissal, finding that the NEPA claims were not moot, since the "engineering phase" of the project would be ongoing for some time. She dismissed the FOIA claims but allowed them to be refiled if a defect were corrected. And she determined that the question of whether the DOE had complied with the Nuclear Non-Proliferation Act and Atomic Energy Act "is a factual question reviewable under the arbitrary and capricious standard"—in other words, a matter subject to the court's jurisdiction.

It had to be an encouraging milestone in a case that, in all other respects, was exhausting and frustrating.

HUMPTY-DUMPTY AT THE DOE

IN EARLY 1996, GREEN WAS ASKING THE COURT FOR PERMISSION TO FILE ANOTHER— the fourth—amended complaint. By now, the list of the various projects associated with the DOE's efforts to reprocess transuranic wastes came to 10 pages. Taken as a whole, they amounted to a unified DOE action that, Green argued, should be subject to a single, comprehensive environmental impact statement, rather than the several smaller environmental assessments that the DOE claimed were sufficient to satisfy the requirements of NEPA.

As the parties were discussing this motion, Green and Hirsch learned of the DOE's intention to proceed, without waiting for any court decision, with treatment of a ton of spent nuclear fuel from an experimental breeder reactor at Argonne National Laboratory—West, in Idaho. On May 16, the DOE gave the plaintiffs part of an environmental assessment and its finding of no significant impact for the project, notifying them as well that it had authorized the Idaho lab to begin operations on May 31, 1996.

Green immediately faxed the DOE's lead attorney a request that the DOE postpone startup of the project until the court had a chance to rule on the merits of the litigation, which sought a broader EIS. The request was rejected, with the DOE's general counsel notifying the plaintiffs that the period between May 16 and May 31 should be adequate to address any concerns.

Green then sought a temporary restraining order from Judge Wilken. With the motion pending, the DOE backed off—a little. The judge had scheduled a June 6 hearing on the motion for the TRO. If it was denied, the DOE said, the project would go forward as planned the next day.

One of the chief objections that Hirsch and others plaintiffs had to TRUMP-S and the ever-growing list of related DOE projects was that they were all aimed at developing new ways of reprocessing spent nuclear fuel. Reprocessing, which involves the separation of high-level radioactive elements, such as plutonium, from radioactive waste, can facilitate the production of nuclear weapons. For this reason, Congress has placed tight controls on the technologies associated with reprocessing, as an issue of national security. In addition, NEPA regulations require an EIS, and not a less comprehensive environmental assessment, for any reprocessing project.

The DOE had insisted that the various projects had nothing to do with reprocessing, but one of the documents that had been disclosed to the plaintiffs effectively gave the lie to the DOE's claim. In 1994, the DOE's Office of Nuclear Energy forwarded to the director of the Idaho Falls lab an "operational readiness review plan of action" for restarting the fuel cycle facility there. "You may want to do a 'reprocessing' word search, just to be safe," the lab director was advised. Sure enough, on pages 6 and 8 of the plan, the word "reprocessing" appears, with a strike-out over the "re."

In asking for the temporary restraining order and preliminary injunction, Green called attention to the DOE's efforts to disguise its project with new terminology. "For years DOE had described this specific project as reprocessing. All of the documents which were in preliminary drafting stage when this decision was made also described this project as reprocessing. When DOE decided that the word should mean something different, DOE had to search all of the draft documents with a computer, to remove the word 'reprocessing.' . . . DOE's posture is reminiscent of Humpty-Dumpty: 'When *I* use a word . . . it means just what I choose it to mean' (emphasis in original)."

Guidelines with a Capital 'G'

Judge Wilken did not grant the TRO. In July, however, she heard arguments on the merits of the case. The Department of Energy attempted to block full EIS review, arguing that the likelihood of eventual success of the various projects (and, by extension, the consequences of such success) was, in any case, highly speculative.

Green countered by attempting to educate Judge Wilken about the potential long-range consequences of success, however slim the chances: "As Your Honor stated in an opinion last summer, the environmental review of these projects must review the purpose—what would happen if they're successful. The DOE can't escape an environmental review of the impact of what it's doing by claiming it'll fail."

The DOE was trying to develop a way to remove the long-lived actinides from nuclear waste, so that what remains could be disposed of in so-called "low-level" waste repositories, Green said. But, he continued, "I trust Your Honor knows, low-level waste does not really mean low-risk waste. Low-level waste is often a lot hotter than some of the high-level waste. Low-level waste is a term that . . . defines waste on the basis of the source that it comes from, not on the basis of how hot the stuff is."

If successful, the Department of Energy would be "putting in the low-level waste dumps, instead of a deep geological depository, great quantities of highly radioactive nuclear waste. The environmental impacts of that have not been considered at all. . . . They're looking at a whole lot of technologies to try to find the ones that will best achieve that goal, and refusing to evaluate the environmental impacts of achieving that goal if they succeed."

Judge Wilken asked why this couldn't proceed on a project-by-project basis.

Green: "It isn't that this project will produce 'x' waste. The project in a laboratory may produce a little bit of waste. That's not the principal concern. The concern is that one or more of these projects will reach a point of development at which they come into general usage, either in this country or elsewhere in the world. . . . The point is that there is this overall program"—Green had identified at least three dozen projects— "which DOE has recognized repeatedly to develop one or more technologies in order to achieve this goal."

Green also raised the point that the DOE's own guidelines prohibited the export of sensitive nuclear technologies to so-called "unsophisticated countries" that were not already in possession of the technologies. The judge, confused, asked the lead attorney from the Department of Justice, Maria Iizuka, about the regulation.

"Now, what do you know about this?" Wilken asked Iizuka. Green "says there's guidelines with a capital 'G' that say that you can't give things to [un]sophisticated countries."

Iizuka professed to know nothing of the regulation, prompting Matt Urie, with the DOE Office of the General Counsel, to insert himself into the proceedings: "A determination on whether technology is sensitive nuclear technology . . . here again, I'm not familiar with the regulations, but it—it may—a technology may be sensitive nuclear technology vis-à-vis one country and perhaps not vis-à-vis another country."

Judge Wilken seemed amazed: "Oh, so you DO do this."

Again, the DOE's attorneys seemed reluctant to commit one way or another on the issue.

"Okay," said the judge, "my impression is, you've been denying that. So I think you need to figure out whether that is or is not part of your definition because he [Green] says, if it is, it's bad."

The government attorneys proceeded to argue that the whole subject was moot, since TRUMP-S did not involve sensitive nuclear technology at all. The judge again expressed dismay: "It wouldn't be sensitive for anybody?" she asked.

Iizuka: "Yes, exactly."

Judge Wilken: "In other words, even without regard to whether it's sophisticated or not, it's not sensitive?"

Iizuka assured her it was not, because "it's a well-known technology."

Containment

Apart from the verbal sparring over DOE guidelines, the fundamental question before the court remained that of compliance with the National Environmental Policy Act. By the time the court got around to hearing arguments on this issue, stages 1 and 2 of the TRUMP-S project had been completed, making moot any question about the sufficiency of the environmental disclosure documents drawn up for them. As for stage 3, the Department of Energy had issued a "categorical exclusion," claiming that under its rules, projects such as this had minimal impact on the environment and thus no EIS or environmental assessment needed to be prepared.

Green disagreed. "The categorical exclusion determination on phase 3 . . . explicitly incorporates by reference the EA and the FONSI [finding of no significant impact] on stages 1 and 2. It takes off from them, says, well, gee, there isn't much difference, we're just going into the engineering phase. I don't think it's a stand-alone document."

In an effort to demonstrate for the judge the trivial scope of the experiments, Iizuka brought out a small ceramic cylinder. "Your Honor, if I might. . . . This is the TRUMP-S project, Your Honor. This is it. . . ."

The judge was aghast. "You've got the nuclear waste right up there?"

Iizuka hastened to explain that the cylinder in her hands was empty, but "the whole project takes place in a cylinder exactly like this one. That—that's the extent of the project."

But the judge was skeptical of her argument that by merely claiming a project was categorically excluded, the agency could avoid preparation of an EA. "You just say, 'I find this to be a categorical exclusion,' period, end of sentence?" she asked.

"Yes," Iizuka answered.

Judge Wilken, however, understood the point Green had been driving home: "I think what he's saying is that this PT [partitioning and transmutation] process will lead to a different and new kind of nuclear waste that you don't know what problems it might have," she said.

Iizuka dismissed the concern: "I don't think so. . . . Even if there were, certainly there would be the ability to contain it, to deal with it—and address the problem at that time. But I think that's not a realistic—it's one of these things that Mr. Green has thrown out from time to time."

Green argued that it was the DOE itself that claimed the waste would be different. "They claim it will be so different, we can put it in low-level waste dumps at the surface level instead of deep geological repositories. . . . That's the goal of the entire separation program here. And the environmental impacts of depositing this terribly hot stuff in low-level waste dumps have never been examined by anybody."

A Settlement

The litigation by this time was entering its sixth year. The experiments at the University of Missouri, which served as the instant cause of the lawsuit, were practically at an end. The California attorney working with Green on the case, William Brockett, Jr., had been incapacitated by brain cancer in September 1995 and from that point to his death in June 1996, was unable to help.

In January 1997, Judge Wilken issued an order upholding the plaintiffs' claims that the DOE's categorical exclusion for the third stage of the

TRUMP-S project was issued in error. The Freedom of Information Act claims, largely satisfied by the DOE's production of documents, albeit grudging and slow, still awaited a decision by the judge, as did the claim of violations of the Nuclear Non-Proliferation Act. But the judge had found in DOE's favor on the key issue of whether an EIS for the entire project was required.

The decision launched settlement talks between Green and Iizuka, the Justice Department attorney.

Iizuka had suggested that the plaintiffs might dismiss the outstanding Nuclear Non-Proliferation Act and Freedom of Information Act claims, in return for which the defendants would "negotiate some reasonable fees and expenses for the litigation of the claims on which the plaintiffs have thus far been successful."

In a letter to Iizuka on January 16, 1997, Green suggested what he described as a 'broader disposition" of the case. The DOE, he suggested, would probably not want Wilken's decision on the categorical exclusion to be established as a precedent. "As we found out in discovery, DOE has issued a number of determinations of categorical exclusion which lacked the findings which the court has held are required. While I don't know how many there are, it seems clear that this ruling points the way to invalidating a substantial number of other DOE determinations of categorical exclusion."

The FOIA determinations to date also might not be something that the DOE would want to stand: "Already other citizens have been contacting us about this ruling," Green told Iizuka. "They are looking for judicial authority to support their claim that DOE must search the records of the contractor . . . as well as the records of the DOE office. Elimination of this precedent should have some appeal to DOE."

Finally, Green said, the NEPA ruling on the programmatic EIS "is clearly erroneous. . . . [T]he ruling of the judge has gotten the facts entirely wrong, and gotten the law quite confused; the ruling looks like a prime candidate for reversal, and the reversal might go a lot farther than DOE wants to go."

"In summary," he wrote, "the January 6 ruling does each side some good, and does each side some harm. I believe that both sides would gain more than they would lose by simply eradicating that ruling."

Hammering out the details, including a modest payment to the plaintiffs, took another three months.

By April 18, 1997, it was all over. The judge approved the settlement and the case was dismissed. In return for dropping their pursuit of the outstanding claims, the plaintiffs had won the DOE's promise that the TRUMP-S experiments would end by September 30 of that year.

Meanwhile, at Mizzou

The long appeal of the amendments to the reactor at the University of Missouri–Columbia to allow the TRUMP-S experiments finally came before the Nuclear Regulatory Commission in 1995. Of the 17 appeals the NRC considered that year, the Mizzou case was the only one that merited a proceeding. To quote the NRC's "Review of Adjudicatory Actions" for 1995, "In that lengthy and complex decision, the Commission essentially affirmed the Presiding Officer's grant of a license for possession and use of material by the University in its TRUMP-S experiments. In addition, the parties in that proceeding filed an unprecedented three rounds of reconsideration petitions."

In 2004, Mizzou asked the NRC to amend its license again, this time to reflect the cessation of the TRUMP-S project. The university "completed experiments at the MURR related to the TRUMP-S Research project on September 30, 1997. By July 20, 1998, [it] had shipped all low-level waste from the project. . . . All transuranic waste (americium, neptunium, and plutonium) was shipped from the MURR to the Waste Isolation Pilot Plant on May 15, 2003."

With that, the TRUMP-S project wound to a close. The legal challenges brought by Green had forced the Department of Energy to disclose thousands of documents revealing the full scope of its efforts to develop new ways of reprocessing irradiated fuel. The settlement did not begin to cover the legal fees and out-of-pocket costs associated with the litigation.

Why did Green take on the case? His wife, Louise, says she always thought it was because visits to the Bay area held out the promise of a dinner at the Tadich Grill. "It was my dad's favorite restaurant in San Francisco," daughter Kathleen Henry said. "He loved the fresh fish there."

CHAPTER 7

A CHALLENGE ON ALL FRONTS AGAINST MOVE OF ARMY CHEMICAL SCHOOL TO MISSOURI

Patricia Tummons

THE DECISION TO TRANSFER THE ARMY'S CHEMICAL WARFARE TRAINING FACILITY from Alabama to Fort Leonard Wood, Missouri, was based on brute political strength. The relative merits of either site had little to do with the decision. Missouri's congressional delegation sought the transfer; Alabama's was opposed to it. Although the Base Realignment and Closure Commission (BRAC), which had to approve the move, was supposed to be blind to such considerations, in the end, it was helpless to do naught but bow to the force of Missouri's superior political muscle.

That, in short, is how Fort Leonard Wood came to host the U.S. Army's only facility to train soldiers in the detection and handling of chemical and biological weapons.

Although the transfer seems in hindsight to have been foreordained, Lewis Green and the clients he represented did manage to reduce the impacts of the new Army facilities. In the process, they won a Missouri Supreme Court victory that has benefited advocates of clean streams ever since.

Along the way, opponents of the transfer were helped a lot, and probably harmed a little, by an alliance of parties with whom they would normally have little in common: a faux grass-roots environmental group, consisting of three public relations professionals; a high-priced Washington lobbying firm; a team of high-profile St. Louis attorneys; and an Alabama electric utility, among others.

AN ALL-OUT CHALLENGE

THE BASE REALIGNMENT AND CLOSURE COMMISSION, ESTABLISHED IN THE 1980S to remove political considerations from Department of Defense decisions on the closure of military facilities, first learned of the Army's plans to move the U.S. Army Chemical School to Fort Leonard Wood in 1991. Any possible opposition on the part of Missouri officials or business leaders was silenced by the Army's threat that if the move didn't happen, the giant Fort Leonard Wood would be shut down. Their support, under those circumstances, was enthusiastic, but BRAC members were reluctant to go along with the plan, since the Army said it would be keeping part of the facility at Fort McClellan, Alabama. In 1993, the Army proposed the transfer again, but commissioners were concerned that it would take years to receive permits to operate the new facilities in Missouri. At that time, the commission warned the Army that if it wanted to bring the proposed move up for consideration a third time, it should make certain that all necessary permits could be received from the state of Missouri in timely fashion.

Throughout 1994, Army officials worked quietly with the Missouri Department of Natural Resources to clear up the BRAC concerns. By December of that year, the deals seem to have been cut. DNR Director David Shorr wrote William J. Perry, the Secretary of Defense, to "reiterate our position regarding permitting at Fort Leonard Wood. As expressed in prior letters, the Missouri Department of Natural Resources has indicated that the CDTF [Chemical Decontamination Training Facility] is a permitable facility under Missouri law. As I indicated on June 4, 1993, we anticipate the construction of this facility will require air pollution control, water pollution control and hazardous waste program-related permits. . . . Missouri is prepared to expedite the review processes for these facilities."

On February 28, 1995, the Army obtained BRAC approval for the move. The next day, the Department of Natural Resources was buried under a pile of applications for the permits—allowing for discharges into streams, for air emissions, and for waste processing—needed to accommodate the relocation of the U.S. Army Chemical School to the rolling wooded foothills of the Ozarks.

There was the application for authority to construct, needed to cover emissions from the "static and mobile fog oil smoke training" operation. The Army claimed these training exercises, intended to simulate combat conditions, would emit 233.73 tons of volatile organic carbons each year.

A permit for hazardous waste was sought to allow for construction of a "thermal treatment unit" that would dispose of hazardous wastes from the Chemical Decontamination Training Facility. Associated with that was an application for a prevention-of-significant-deterioration permit, intended to insure that air pollution from the incinerator would be limited.

Application was made to the DNR's Clean Water Commission for an amendment to Fort Leonard Wood's National Pollutant Discharge Elimination System (NPDES) permit, which regulates the release of pollutants into streams.

True to its word, the DNR acted quickly to approve the applications. By mid-April 1995, the DNR had issued permission to construct the Chemical Decontamination Training Facility, had amended the NPDES permit as requested, had given preliminary approval for the smoke training operations, and had determined that no permit was actually required for the hazardous waste incinerator.

The actions paved the way for legal challenges by the Missouri Coalition for the Environment, the Missouri chapter of the Sierra Club, and several individuals living near Fort Leonard Wood. Representing them all was Green.

THE ALABAMA CONNECTION

THE PETITIONS SEEKING TO OVERTURN THE PERMITS WERE BASED ON AN extensive—and expensive—study of the technical aspects associated with the Army's proposed operations, prepared by the engineering consulting firm of Schreiber, Grana & Yonley, Inc., of St. Louis. Between the time the Army sought the permits and the filing of the legal challenges, the firm had examined every angle of the claims made and supporting materials provided in an effort to hone in on potential weaknesses, contradictions, or omissions.

The results were impressive: a binder of more than 700 pages that found fault with the Army's analyses, took exception to many of its claims, and disputed some of the approaches to permitting that the Army and DNR had taken.

The question arises: How could the Coalition, which is perennially run on a shoestring budget, the cash-strapped Missouri chapter of the Sierra Club, and the several individuals who mounted the challenges possibly afford the services of professional consultants?

The answer: They didn't need to. The Schreiber Grana report was paid for by a group of Alabama businesses, including the Anniston Chamber of Commerce and, far and away the biggest contributor, Alabama Power. In addition to the consulting engineers, the group had also retained a law firm in Alabama, a lobbying consultant in Washington, two public relations teams in Missouri, and a public opinion pollster in Michigan. The Alabama legal team had in turn hooked up with one of the largest law firms in St. Louis—Armstrong, Teasdale, Schlafly & Davis.

The Alabama connection brought benefits: there was the engineering report, of course, and a public opinion survey showing how uninformed Missouri residents were of the environmental issues attending the Army move.

But it also made for some uncomfortable moments. The public relations professionals in Missouri had set up a group called PEER (People for Enforcing Environmental Regulations), which attempted to pass itself off as a grass-roots organization. According to an article in the *St. Louis Post-Dispatch,* "Ken Midkiff of the Sierra Club said PEER had represented itself as 'concerned citizens' when it approached the club. Midkiff balked when he later learned it was an Alabama front group. 'I was never told they were receiving money for this,' he said. 'I just quit taking their calls.' Roger Pryor of the Coalition for the Environment said his group 'benefited from the Alabama largess' by using technical advice supplied by PEER.

"When members of Pryor's group testified recently at a hearing on the base move, a legislator criticized them as being 'on the Alabama dole.'

"'I don't feel manipulated,' said Pryor. 'We're doing what we would be doing anyway. We have limited staff.' . . . Both Midkiff and Pryor emphasized that they had not been offered and would not have accepted money from PEER."

Wendy Pelton, a petitioner who lived near Fort Leonard Wood, was aware of the involvement of Alabama interests in the legal maneuverings opposing the transfer, which caused her a great deal of unease. In a letter to Green in June 1995, she objected to even the passing mention of Alabama—or, as she phrased it, Green's "use of the 'A' word over my not-so-private phone line."

"In south central Missouri, it's most certainly a curse word," she informed Green in the same letter. "Although I have acknowledged to the world, via reporters, that I have eagerly and gratefully received and sought out lots of accurate and thorough information from folks with 'A' funding, I don't think I want the world to think that my attorney bases his decisions on what 'they' want. . . . I prefer to stay in my blissfully naïve state that believes that you are working for and being paid by the Missouri Coalition for the Environment, who has generously allowed me to join the legal actions at no cost. . . . I don't want to have to face a moral dilemma about doing the right thing with the wrong money."

Any discomfort the environmentalists experienced, however, must have paled alongside that experienced by Ken Teasdale, a partner in the St. Louis law firm working with the Alabama coalition. Teasdale, a close political ally of Governor Mel Carnahan, was in Carnahan's office on April 13, when, as he wrote the next day in a memo to all lawyers in the firm, the governor and two aides informed him "that they had heard reports that our firm had been retained to represent interests in Alabama in an effort to have these military activities transferred to bases in Alabama rather than in Missouri."

Teasdale went on to say that he had "assured the Governor . . . that I was not aware of any such representation, although some kind of group or company that would have an unfamiliar name might have come through on one of the conflict notices. I assured the governor that we would not take any such representation contrary to the interests of the governor and the state of Missouri should we be approached concerning such a representation. . . . If you have any information regarding this, please advise me immediately as I must report to the governor's office as quickly as possible concerning this matter."

On the very day Teasdale drafted the memo, Richard Waters of Armstrong Teasdale was conducting a strategy session in the law firm's St. Louis boardroom. Issues to be discussed reportedly included administrative opportunities to attack the permits Missouri had issued to the Army to accommodate the transfer, hazardous waste issues, factual issues, citizen suits under the Endangered Species Act, the Clean Air Act, the Clean Water Act, and the Resource Conservation and Recovery Act. Until it became clear that the transfer was not going to be undone, lawyers from the Armstrong firm would be involved in challenging the move.

For lawyers and lobbyists more accustomed to working on behalf of corporate polluters, the experience of fighting side by side with environmentalists must have been a novelty. When the Alabama interests pulled out in August 1995, lobbyists with the Hawthorne Group in Washington reflected on their shared experiences in a memo to Edward Noel, an Armstrong attorney: "While being on the 'side of the angels' may have been a new experience for most of us, the unexpected benefit of engaging in such a fight is the opportunity to develop new colleagues and friendships.... Here's hoping we get the opportunity to do it again."

CHAOS

PERMITTING FOR THE SMOKE TRAINING EXERCISES POSED A PROBLEM. UNDER Missouri opacity rules, emissions from new regulated activities must not impair visibility more than 20 percent. While exceptions were allowed for some purposes (private barbecues and charcoal kilns, for example), no provision existed that would allow the Air Conservation Commission to issue a variance for the Army's obscurant training operations, which were intended to produce 100 percent opacity. Variances could be issued only when enforcement of the opacity rule would result in a taking of property or the closing or elimination of a business, occupation, or activity.

But the DNR asked the Air Conservation Commission for a variance for the Army fog training anyway. On April 27, 1995, Green promptly petitioned on behalf of opponents for a full hearing on the variance issue before the commission. In an effort to accommodate the DNR and the Army, the commission scheduled a hearing—for May 25, less than a month away.

On May 3, Green asked the commission to appoint a hearing officer, to allow a continuance, and to consolidate the petition on the variance request for the fog training with an appeal of the authority to construct that the DNR had issued for the CDTF incinerator. His request was denied, and over the next three weeks, Green had to arrange and conduct depositions of a dozen witnesses in addition to preparing the case for presentation to the commission by the end of the month.

The issues before the commission were limited to two questions: whether granting a variance would create a health problem and whether denial would result in the prohibition of a lawful activity "without sufficient corresponding benefit or advantage to the people," wrote assistant attorney general Deborah Neff, representing the DNR. "Not granting the variance will prohibit the training from occurring," Neff wrote. "Fort Leonard Wood contends that the training is necessary for national security reasons."

The two weeks before the hearing were chaotic, Green later wrote. "In the week of May 15–19, 1995, depositions were taken every day for twelve to thirteen hours per day. Monday, May 22, was a day free of depositions because of the conflicting schedule of counsel for the Army. On May 23, depositions were scheduled to commence at 10 a.m. They continued to 1:30 a.m. on May 24. After 1:30 a.m., the court reporters had to work throughout the night to get the transcript to the airport for counsel for the Army on the morning of May 24."

What transpired during the MACC hearing was, if anything, even more tumultuous. "The hearing officer failed to preside over the proceedings and permitted the hearing to degenerate into chaos," Green wrote in the inevitable appeal of the decision to Circuit Court in St. Louis. "From the beginning, other commissioners took over and directed the hearing. One commissioner . . . was especially dominant, directing proceedings constantly. A commissioner on her left tried unsuccessfully to compete. These individuals [took] full control over the hearing, freely castigating counsel and ruling on motions, objections, and various procedural matters. . . . The two became partisans, arguing against plaintiffs even when no objection had been made. Chaos prevailed, even before the two disagreed with one another, leaving plaintiffs' counsel in a quandary. Repeatedly plaintiffs' counsel was compelled to plead for a clear ruling so that he could comply with whatever the ruling might be. Through it all, the hearing officer maintained a posture of benign neglect. When roused to activity she would utter her routine ruling: objection sustained, even when no objection had been made."

Given the circus atmosphere that prevailed during the hearing, the decision that emerged in June could have been no surprise to Green: the variance was granted, even though the Army was never able to say exactly what the fog oil would be composed of, whether it would include hazardous air pollutants, or when, how often, and under what circumstances fogging would be permitted.

On March 26, 1996, Judge Robert H. Dierker, Jr., vacated the variance and remanded the issue to the Air Conservation Commission with instructions that it reopen the record to allow further cross-examination of witnesses. "Although the conduct of the hearing . . . was not a model of orderly procedure," Dierker wrote, "the court detects no reversible error in the chairman's failure to exercise stricter control over procedural rulings. . . . [T]he haphazard way in which commission members in this case injected themselves into procedural objections during the hearing does not warrant reversal."

Still, he continued, "the commission's restrictions on the scope of cross-examination by petitioners and the exclusion of petitioners' proffered deposition testimony at the hearing were erroneous. . . . [T]his abuse of discretion by the commission would not lead to reversal in this case, but for the concomitant error of excluding all evidence pertaining to health hazard."

None of the parties was pleased with Dierker's order. The two parties represented by Green, Wendy Pelton and the Coalition for the Environment, appealed, contending that the court erred in its determination that the commission had the authority to issue a variance, among other things. The Army, the commission, and the DNR appealed as well.

But the appeals were deemed moot. To address the specific case of the fog training, the DNR had changed its rules, issuing first an emergency exemption for the Army from the opacity rule in July 1995, and then making the exception permanent by October of that year.

Green and other attorneys involved in the variance hearing and litigation were able to petition for fees. Green sought nearly $100,000 for his time, plus travel costs of around $4,400 and consultant costs of more than $150,000, while attorneys for Armstrong Teasdale sought $37,000 for all expenses. Dierker granted in total an insulting $37,000.

There were other air permits as well relating to the authority to construct the obscurant training facility and an incinerator, both challenged by Green and his clients, the Missouri Coalition for the Environment and Wendy Pelton. The appeals were little more than speed bumps thrown in the path of the Army, although at least one of them did in fact change the nature of the Army's eventual operations. For example, in the face of trouble winning approvals of the proposed hazardous waste incinerator associated with the CDTF, the Army simply dropped plans for that facility and pledged to ship hazardous wastes offsite.

During the course of the appeals, state regulators and the Army seemed to conspire against Green and his clients. Hearings on the appeals were stayed while the Army figured out conditions it would actually be operating under—and when it finally did, the state simply issued a new permit rather than amending the ones being challenged. With the original permits now superseded, the appeals were deemed moot. When in September 2002, Green, recovering from heart surgery, missed an appeal deadline of the new permit by a few days, no further appeal was possible.

OVERTURNING CRAVEN

THE ARMY'S TRANSFER OF ITS CHEMICAL SCHOOL FROM ALABAMA TO MISSOURI was, in the end, unstoppable. Yet one important legal victory emerged from the challenges that Green mounted against the move, and that was the overturning by the Missouri Supreme Court of a lower court decision that had effectively denied third parties the right to challenge permits issued under Missouri's clean-water law by bringing administrative (non-judicial) appeals.

Among the permits needed by the Army was an amended NPDES permit for Fort Leonard Wood, since the new activities would be increasing the pollutants released into Missouri streams. In 1999, the director of the Department of Natural Resources issued the permit, but the Missouri Coalition for the Environment and three individuals appealed, asking the Clean Water Commission to review the action.

As the appeal was pending before the commission, the Missouri

Court of Appeals, Western District, handed down a decision in *Craven v. State ex rel. Premium Standard Farms, Inc.*—a case where a neighbor had sought to appeal an operating permit issued to two hog "confinement farms." Such facilities contain thousands of hogs whose manure is stored in lagoons. The lagoon waste is sprayed on nearby fields and eventually ends up in streams and lakes that were used recreationally by members of the public.

The Western District Court of Appeals had determined that the commission could hear appeals of permits only from parties whose requests for permits had been denied. As a result, the Clean Water Commission dismissed all third-party appeals before it, including the Coalition's appeal of the Fort Leonard Wood permit.

The Coalition then appealed to the Circuit Court of the City of St. Louis, which agreed with the Western District Appeals Court and, on July 25, 2002, dismissed the Coalition's suit.

On September 3, Green filed notice of appeal to the Missouri Court of Appeals, Eastern District. And barely a month later, he was pushing the Missouri Supreme Court to take the case, even before the lower court had heard arguments and made its decision. The action was warranted, he wrote, "because of the need for a prompt resolution by this court of a question of administrative procedure which is of the greatest importance in the administration of Missouri's clean water law."

The Supreme Court didn't bite. And so, in the spring of 2003, Green found himself preparing for oral arguments before the appeals court.

They were arguments he would not get a chance to make.

When the court finally heard the case, on June 10, it was Green's daughter, Kathleen Henry, who represented the Coalition.

"I regret that I am here as a pinch hitter for my father, Lewis Green," Henry told the court. "He passed away on May 16. He had a unique style of oration that I cannot hope to replicate. In addition, he very much wanted to conduct this argument. At the beginning of April, he told me to start preparing the research for it. He was very concerned about the *Craven* decision and its ramifications."

The appeals court agreed in a ruling issued June 30, 2003, remanding the permit appeal to the Clean Water Commission "for a hearing on the merits." The commission was now in a bind, with two appellate court decisions giving it conflicting instructions.

The state attorney general then asked that the case be transferred to the Missouri Supreme Court. The court quickly agreed to take it up, with Kathleen Henry making the case for the Coalition. In its decision, handed down July 1, 2004, Green's arguments were vindicated. Missouri law, the court determined, "grants those denied a permit the right to appeal to the commission, and any person with an interest that is or may be adversely affected by a permit decision is permitted to appeal to the community. . . . [The statute] does not limit the right of appeal to the commission solely to those denied a permit. . . . Therefore, the commission has subject matter jurisdiction to hear the coalition's appeal. The judgment is reversed and the case is remanded."

The victory is an important one in the history of Missouri clean-water regulation, but the practical effect on activities at Fort Leonard Wood was nil. The Great Rivers Environmental Law Center, the non-profit group that Green had established shortly before his death, was able to recover some legal fees. But by the time the Supreme Court made its decision, the Army's Chemical Decontamination Training Facility was in full operation.

"After the *Craven* case came down, the Coalition for the Environment had no funds to hire experts, which would have been necessary to appeal the permit," Henry said. "The Coalition had undergone a huge change during the period of the Fort Leonard Wood litigation. Bruce [Morrison, who litigated the case with Henry] and I could not find free experts. So it is kind of a sad ending, but it was a good verdict in the Supreme Court."

CHAPTER 8

A RIVERBOAT GAMBLE IN
THE COURTS SAVES A PRECIOUS
SLICE OF NATURE

Florence Shinkle

ON SUNDAY, DECEMBER 15, 2002, A FEW WEEKS AFTER LEWIS GREEN GAVE $600,000 of his own money to establish Great Rivers Environmental Law Center, the first law firm in St. Louis solely dedicated to public interest environmental litigation in St. Louis, a profile of him appeared in the *St. Louis Post-Dispatch* written by environmental reporter Sara Shipley. In it, Green traced his passion for public interest law to a near-death experience in 1959.

Somehow he had contracted encephalitis, the often-fatal brain-swelling disease, and he'd been in a coma for two weeks.

Shipley wrote, "But no one wanted to give up on the promising young attorney. His father's law clients stopped by. Friends donated thousands of dollars and requested that masses were said in Green's name, even though he wasn't Catholic. Someone bought a $5000 respirator the hospital needed to treat him.

"When Green finally struggled to consciousness, he learned how his friends came to his aid. And that, he says, is when he decided to devote the rest of his life to public service.

"'I figured I ought to pay something back,'" Green said.

It is a dramatic account of the root cause behind a life of public service, a coming-to-consciousness story that must have made the reporter inwardly rejoice at its readiness for print. In fact, it is so dramatic, so neatly explanatory that you'd think Green would have illuminated it earlier to his wife, Louise, or to some of the attorneys who practiced with him, if only to quell further probing by them.

But when the story appeared as the lead in Shipley's article, most of his closest associates were bemused.

"Well, yes, I guess that could have been true," Louise Green said accommodatingly, weighing the information against what she knew of the man. "He could have got his direction then. I know that after he served as a (Democratic) committeeman (in Kirkwood) and [former Governor Warren] Hearnes got in, he asked Hearnes to give him some sort of environmental appointment. I don't think he cared what."

Rick Lageson, who graduated from law school in 1975 and worked at Green, Hennings and Henry until 1982, says Green never related to him the "wakeup call" story he told reporter Shipley. Asked for his best thinking on Green's motivations for practicing environmental law, Lageson obligingly provided a number of factors ranging from temperament to upbringing to simple opportunity. Like Everest, the field was there, with a magnetic pull for someone who needed a mighty engagement against which to test himself.

That Green would practice law, like his father and grandfather whose firm was founded in 1877, was evidently a given of his childhood; so the question was how he would practice, in pursuit of what goals and in what setting. Despite allergies and a breathing problem, he grew into a tall, handsome man of great physical and intellectual vigor, with no tolerance for mediocrity, unquestionably a man who needed his intellectual autonomy. Louise Green says her husband was always determined to run his own ship and avoid a lot of bosses muddying his briefs.

Lageson tells the following anecdote about Green's limited ability to tolerate fools: "Once after a case we'd lost but should have won, I said to Lew about the judge we'd dealt with, 'Yeah, but Lew he's a nice guy.'

"And Lew snorted, 'Nice guy! My dog is a nice guy! That doesn't mean he should be adjudicating our rights and responsibilities under the law!'"

So he set out to be his own boss. Undoubtedly, he also set out to practice some sort of socially significant law of equal importance with his father's First Amendment practice. John Raeburn Green had handled

First Amendment cases for the *St. Louis Post-Dispatch*. The paternal presence was a felt thing in the office. On the wall was a plaque with the editorial the *Post* published on the death of the elder Green in 1973.

Lageson: "When that First Amendment work wasn't there anymore, I think Lew started looking for something comparable. He definitely needed something more to do than that wills-and-bills of a general practice. He got a kick out of tweaking the stuffy powers that be, and he enjoyed a solitary battle against dug-in interests."

The National Environmental Policy Act was passed in 1969, the same year that Green exited the Clean Air Commission. The Clean Water Act was approved in 1972. The opportunity to test the power of these acts and become a guiding legal presence in the emerging field of environmental law would not have been lost on this ambitious man. He accepted the post of attorney for the Missouri Coalition for the Environment. He had found his arena, his vocation, a type of law that suited his warrior's nature and his outsized sense of legal duty. After that, his legal life proceeded on two tracks; the chug-chug of the routine money-earning cases played out alongside the great battles for the environment.

"He Liked Being a Lawyer"

YET EVEN THE CASES TAKEN PRIMARILY FOR FEES RECEIVED AN ALL-OUT EFFORT from Green. Jud Calkins, a *Post-Dispatch* reporter turned attorney, recalls a custody case against Green: "He did not have the good set of facts. WE had the good set of facts. But he would not give up. He would not quit. He was a very ambitious, aggressive trial attorney and I would bet he fought every battle totally, the same way he fought that custody case. It was something he had to do for himself."

Lageson recalls that no work left the firm until Lew Green approved the quality, no matter how prolonged the delays to get things right.

"One thing we did not do in that firm," Lageson said, with the certainty of a man uttering an ultimate truth, "we did not practice law for money."

One look at the cozy, shabby office told any visitor the same thing. The Greens were not in law for the money. They were in it for the spiritual side, although Lew Green would have pooh-poohed such an assertion as pure treacle. Nevertheless, anyone who knew Lew Green knew he lived for the legal battle well fought.

Edward Heisel, formerly legal policy director for the Coalition for the Environment, now executive director of Ozark Regional Land Trust, believes Green's endurance in the midst of so many discouraging rulings derived from his understanding that he was doing what he was intended to do: "'I think first and foremost he liked being a lawyer. He liked the game of it and didn't seem to develop any ulcers by the sometimes gut-wrenching decisions that had to be made or from the stern warnings from developers' attorneys," Heisel wrote in a reminiscent e-mail of September 27, 2008. "He seemed to take all this in stride understanding it as part of the game, even enjoying it a lot of the time. If you have this perspective, and also believe that victories come in different shapes and sizes, then it does not seem like so much tilting at windmills. Instead, you're part of the process and if you weren't there, then the process wouldn't work. There are dozens, perhaps hundreds of lawyers and lobbyists on the other side for every one on our side. They would run amok if someone wasn't looking over their shoulder. For every one lawsuit filed by the Coalition, its presence probably avoids the need for another nine."

Green was not a traditionally religious man but he was religious in his commitment to practicing law for the right reasons. And as long as he did so, he was buoyant, defeats be damned. Four years after her husband's death, Louise Green was surprised when she read histories of cases Green had contested and learned of the many adverse rulings. "Lew was always so upbeat," she said. "I assumed we must be doing so well."

By the standards he set for himself, Lewis Green was doing well. He had mobilized all his talents in behalf of a cause greater than himself. He was fulfilling his family's expectation for himself. And, whether he was familiar with the Book of Job or not, he was doing as the Bible instructed: "Thou shalt be in league with the stones in the field."

A lawyer could justifiably be upbeat over fulfilling that commandment and its companion one: "And the beasts of the field shall be at peace with thee" (Job 5:23).

MONEY, IN BALANCE

CHOOSING PRINCIPLE OVER MONEY WAS PRETTY EASY FOR GREEN MOST OF THE time. He appreciated money—"We never ignored a good fee," Lageson said—but he never let money use him. There were cases in which he was criticized for happily accepting cash from interests that he normally might have challenged in court. For instance, when he mounted a challenge against Mills shopping center being built on the Hazelwood bottoms, he happily took financing for the case from Westfield Shopping Centers, a big competing operation. The story made headlines: The environmental movement was accepting big bucks from commercial developers, sleeping with the enemy as it were. Green shrugged and grinned. The money was being used for good intent, so why the outcry as if there were an ethics violation?

"It seems like the first thing you do is go to competitors who might support a lawsuit," he dismissed the issue in a *Post-Dispatch* article of October 2002. "It's the natural thing."

Meanwhile, Hazelwood Mayor T. R. Carr, who wanted the tax dollars from the incoming mall, sermonized, "It's inappropriate for Westfield to hide behind a local community environmental organization to protect a near monopoly of shopping centers in the St. Louis region."

By the time of that flap, Green knew his own imperviousness to financial temptation. A few years earlier, he had been tested by a particularly alluring money offer, calibrated to his heart's desire. In 1995, riverboat gambling entrepreneurs made a subtle, devilish attempt to get environmentalists to trade principle for cash. The money offer came from businessmen who wanted to dock a casino boat at Riverwoods Park, the 123-acre strip of undeveloped land that was given to the public as part of the settlement of the Earth City lawsuit.

Missourians approved riverboat gambling on the Missouri and Mississippi rivers in November 1992. While the Legislature wrangled over what types of games would be allowed and what betting limits imposed on gamblers, the casino developers arrived to stake out territories. And for those in a position to fulfill their commercial longings, money rained down like waters.

For instance, North Shore Casinos wanted to put a casino-theater-hotel complex along the Mississippi River north of Interstate 270. The dealmakers in that group promised St. Louis County $250,000 when it began investigating the license application, $250,000 on opening, and $1 million annually if they got dealt a good hand. Casino America, Inc., preferred a site on the Missouri River at U.S. Highway 67, and that interest group offered St. Louis County a flat $1 million when it opened, plus 1 percent of the revenues annually after taxes.

In May 1994, the Missouri Gaming Commission greenlighted the first two operations. The vintage *Admiral* excursion boat on the Mississippi at St. Louis found new life as the President's Casino and on the Missouri at St. Charles, Station Casinos opened St. Charles Riverfront Station.

A Precious Place

ACROSS THE RIVER FROM RIVERFRONT STATION ON THE ST. LOUIS COUNTY BANK was Riverwoods public area, a wild strip of scrub and sand that survived like an artifact of what the undeveloped river bottoms had once been. Green and the Coalition had obtained the area for public recreation in return for relinquishing the suit to block Earth City, the first major development in the St. Louis County flood plain. Riverwoods was not an elegantly pastoral place, but it was precious, a remaining fold of sunset-occupied sky and earth surrounded by a dead sea of concrete.

The consent decree specified that Crow Development, the owner of Earth City in 1976 when the settlement was approved, would "maintain the area as an unimproved natural green belt area along the river ... to be used without charge by members of the public ... for purposes of hiking, birdwatching, nature observation, family picnics and fishing."

One exceptional activity was permitted by the decree: "The defendant Crow-St. Louis Industrial Inc. reserves whatever rights it may have to remove dirt or fill from the specified area for use in the Earth City development, to emplace a large barge terminal facility on the riverfront of the specified area for use in the Earth City development and to install appropriate facilities for the purpose of moving any gaseous, liquid or solid materials from Earth City development across the specified area to the barge terminal facility."

In other words, Crow kept port rights to haul construction materials in and out.

The right was never exercised. Crow never needed it. But eyeing the site, gambling entrepreneurs saw that clause as a giant loophole in the restrictive uses outlined for Riverwoods, a loophole big enough to drive a riverboat through.

The interested consortium, called Harbor Venture, was a partnership of Thomas Construction, a local construction and landowning company, with two affluent, ingratiating casino developers, Jack Binion, originator of the World Series of Poker and a son of legendary Nevada casino operator Benny Binion, and Don Schupak, a New York lawyer with enormous wealth from sports broadcasting deals.

If these two were convinced everyone had his price, it was probably something they'd learned from experience.

After a fight with his siblings over who got to control Horseshoe Casino, their father's venerable gambling operation in Las Vegas, the affable Jack Binion had shrewdly settled for the expansion rights to Horseshoe's business outside Nevada boundaries. Sure enough, one by one, other states approved gambling for the tax revenues. By the time he arrived in Missouri, Binion already had boats operating in Louisiana and Mississippi. He took one look at the site at Riverwoods across from St. Charles Station Casino and rejoiced to *Post-Dispatch* reporter Fred Faust, "I've kissed a lot of frogs the last couple of years looking for deals. We've found three handsome princes, and this is one of them." (The other two were in southern Indiana and Milford, Conn.)

Donald Schupak was less colorful but more deft, a straightforward, extremely tenacious dealmaker. He was a former owner of the defunct American Basketball League. When the league dissolved, he and his partners got the four surviving teams into the National Basketball League. In return for the rescue, the partners received one/seventh of the four teams' television receipts in perpetuity. Some estimates of the windfall topped $100 million. How did the deal get done? "Mr. Schupak pushed it through. Mr. Schupak just wore everybody out," Mike Goldberg, the counsel for the American Basketball group, told the *Wall Street Journal* in an article published February 22, 1999.

The group's $111 million proposal for Riverwoods included: a five-deck cruising boat with 30,000 square feet of gaming space; a permanently moored barge with 14,000 square feet of gaming space at the riverbank in the conservation area; and a moving covered walkway across the conservation area to ferry disembarking boat passengers to a 200-room hotel and parking lots on the protected side of the levee.

This immense gaming complex was permitted under terms of the consent decree, investors declared, by the permissive clause allowing barge mooring. What was pathetic was the number of political and professional leaders eager to agree with that interpretation of the consent degree's intent, including the officers of the Missouri Department of Conservation, the current owner of Riverwoods.

State Stewardship

In 1984, the MDOC had accepted Riverwoods through a deed of dedication from Ford Motor Credit Company, ending private management of the strip by a successive number of Earth City developers. The dedication had allowed only site improvements compatible with land in "an unimproved natural state," eliminating any reference to barge parking contained in the original consent decree.

"Of course, we were thrilled when the Conservation Department took over control. Right away they started making trails and trying to keep out the 4-wheels. We breathed a sigh of relief," recalled John Nichols, a member of the Coalition for the Environment who was a plaintiff in the Earth City lawsuit that led to the establishment of the park. "And then they got offered these vast sums by the gambling interests and that was that."

Jerry Presley, the director of the agency, would later claim in court that his department had been evaluating its isolated properties since 1990 to weigh their public traffic and unique features against the difficulty of maintaining them. The study had determined that Riverwoods "had no particular unique features and some management difficulties" from illegal use of the park by four-wheelers. So the agency decided, in 1995 after the gambling groups had arrived and expressed interest, to offer the property for sale.

But money, not the difficulty of maintaining the property, was clearly the chief motivator.

The MDOC received three bids for the property. Station Casinos, the gambling company operating a boat on the St. Charles side of the river, teamed with the city of St. Charles to offer $300,000, plus $100 an acre plus title to 14 acres of wetlands near West Alton.

Clayton Investment Corp. offered simply $8,000 an acre.

And Harbor Venture, the casino development corporation formed by Horseshoe owner Binion and Schupak's Missouri River Equities, offered $200,000 for an option, $100,000 a year to extend the option for a maximum of four years, plus a purchase price of $1.4 million when the sale went through.

On April 14, 1995, no surprise, the four-member Missouri Conservation Commission voted unanimously to award the sale of Riverwoods to Harbor Venture.

"That's fine, we'll just have to haul their ass into federal court now," snapped Roger Pryor, head of the Coalition, to the *St. Charles Journal*.

Letters protesting the MDOC's sale of the property, written by Ted House, senator for the Second District, and Steve Ehlmann, then senator for the 23rd District and now chief executive for St. Charles County, got soothing responses from MDOC director Presley. "The deed restrictions you mentioned would accompany the property and ensure its continued availability for public use and green space," he wrote.

But statements by Shannon Cave, public relations officer for the MDOC, dance delicately around the matter of whether the department approved of the uses proposed for Riverwoods by Missouri River Equities. They imply the department knew it was releasing the area to owners who would degrade it but sold it anyway.

"DANGLING BUNDLES OF CASH"

THE MDOC DID NOT NECESSARILY AGREE WITH THE USE PROPOSED BY MISSOURI River Equities, Cave told the *St. Charles Journal*: "There's no agreement on our part to say, 'Go on; build a casino.' There are differences between the way the Conservation Commission interprets the easements on the property and the way the new owners do."

And a letter from Presley to Don Schupak, who was the front man for Harbor Venture, makes clear Presley's chief interest in the deal:

"Further to several conversations we have had with respect to the $1.6 million the Conservation Commission hopes to receive when your gaming project is licensed, I am writing to confirm that it would be the intention of our staff to recommend to our Commission that we reinvest all or a substantial portion of those funds in support of open space or other programs in or around St. Louis County."

The *Post-Dispatch* editorialized about the deal: "Roger Pryor, the Coalition's executive director, must feel like American Indians who discovered that land agreements are made to be broken, especially when money's at stake."

The Conservation Commission's decision to sell Riverwoods left the Coalition with two possible avenues for legal redress—in state court contesting the Conservation Commission's right to sell land dedicated to the agency for public use, and in federal court, defending the intent of the consent decree that originally set aside the acreage as a natural area.

Lew Green being Lew Green and not interested in half-measures, he prepared to file in both venues.

Filed April 4, 1995, the suit in the state circuit court of Cole County, home of the Conservation Commission, challenged the commission's authority to sell the property conveyed to their protection and sought an injunction against the sale, arguing that acceptance of the deed of dedication imposed an obligation to maintain the land for the public.

The commission's attorney Thomas Vetter filed a motion for summary judgment the next month, and while the parties were still in discovery, Cole County Circuit Judge Thomas Brown, in July, ruled in favor of the motion. Brown ruled that the deed of dedication conveying the property to the MDOC had done no more than reiterate the public rights to access already granted out by the federal consent decree of 1976. Since the deed of dedication did not create a new right for the public beyond those that already existed, it did not meet the standard for a true dedication.

"The execution of the deed did not demonstrate a purpose. . . . Rather, it merely reiterated the restrictions set forth in the federal decree and conveyed the property to the Commission," the court ruled.

On appeal, Green blasted the semantics game and its attendant dismissal of the Conservation Commission's responsibility toward donated properties. He pointed out that the dodge "will have a devastating impact on the ability of the state to acquire lands for the public.

"In essence, the court has ruled that an entity which is holding property for public use . . . cannot dedicate the property to the state. . . . According to the court, the State is free to scrap the covenant and sell the property when a riverboat gambler dangles a bundle of cash before the State."

The true test of dedication was intent, Green argued, the intent of the giver and the receiver. And the intent for protection and public benefit was clear in the deed of dedication.

His good arguments got him nowhere. All tiers of the state justice system were determined to affirm the MDOC's authority to sell and buy lands, a right, MDOC attorney Vetter argued, granted in the state constitution. No one outside of the Coalition cared much for the preservation of 123 acres of frequently flooded scrubland, not when it was worth $1.6 million as a boat docking spot.

On July 18, 1995, the Cole County Circuit Court entered its judgment. On August 27, 1996, a panel of the appeals court affirmed it. A motion for rehearing was denied October 1, 1996. The Missouri Supreme Court transferred the case back to the appeals court March 25, 1997, and the appeals court reinstated its previous affirmation of the circuit court ruling April 4, 1997.

A TEMPTING OFFER

THAT EVERY DOOR IN THE STATE SYSTEM HAD SLAMMED SHUT IN SUCCESSION apparently surprised no one. After the initial reports that the circuit court had upheld the MDOC's right to dispose of Riverwoods, scarcely a mention of the progress of the case appears in any of the newspapers that normally covered the environmental movement. It was no news that the state court system upheld the state agency against the wacky environmentalists.

"I went with Lew to Jefferson City to argue to get the case transferred to the Supreme Court. But of course, it just wasn't going to happen," recalled co-plaintiff John Nichols, as resigned to the outcome as everyone else.

The most hopeful arena for environmentalists was the federal courts, where the consent decree had been fashioned. Lew Green knew that. And the Horseshoe Casino and Missouri River Equities group knew it, too.

Donald Schupak of Missouri River Equities mounted a campaign to buy peace. He was way above outright bribing. He knew how to couch his lucrative offers in terms of the public good the money could accomplish. It had worked with the MDOC. Presley, director of the MDOC, couldn't wait to write Schupak about all the natural beauty he was going to buy for the public with the money Schupak was giving for Riverwoods.

So, Schupak tried the same tactic again on the Coalition.

On June 17, 1995, under the byline of reporter Mark Schlinkmann, the *Post-Dispatch* carried the following story:

"A prospective casino developer is seeking to appease environmentalists who have gone to court to block its Earth City project.

"Developers of the Horseshoe Casino Hotel resort are promising to set up a foundation, which would hold $500,000 to $1,000,000 a year in casino revenues to spend on land conservation and other environmental causes . . . if the Coalition would drop its suit."

Schupak didn't fool around with small offers. He dazzled with his generosity: he would give 40 acres of Riverwoods to St. Louis County with $250,000 to maintain it in its natural state. If the casino's after-tax gross revenues exceeded $100 million a year, the foundation's take would grow beyond $1 million according to a sliding formula. But guaranteed for impoverished environmental causes was that $1 million a year. And since the Coalition for the Environment was the only major environmental organization in the region, even though the foundation would have a board that included appointees by the county executive of St. Louis County, it was hard to imagine the Coalition's projects not getting the major funding.

What's strange is how little board members of the Coalition recall about the lucrative offer. The big money apparently didn't register with them.

"I don't remember a thing about it," Arlene Sandler said in a phone call.

"I remember everyone getting together and talking about the clause (in the consent decree) that permitted a barge to operate there for awhile, and we all agreed a barge was not a gambling boat," Rebecca Wright mused.

On November 15, 1995, Lewis Green sent the following letter to opposing counsel Martin Green turning down the offer of $1 million annu-
ally in return for not litigating:

*I appreciate Donald's (Schupak) efforts to develop some sort of
accommodation. I believe he has proceeded in good faith and indicated a desire to be entirely reasonable.*

*However, as I told you before we even met to discuss this, these
controversies are very difficult to settle. A business dispute can often
be settled with dollars, but a dispute over principle is much more
difficult to resolve. I have discussed Donald's proposals with my
clients, and I have explained to them that they will not necessarily
win whatever litigation may be brought. Their response is that they
believe the 1976 consent decree protects the area between the river
from the very kind of development which Donald plans, and they
are unwilling to give up any of that protection.*

*Accordingly, I think we will just have to litigate. Please tell Donald
that I very much appreciate his courtesy and his very reasonable
approach to the disagreement, but I see no way that we can put a
settlement together.*

A Federal Case

On February 1, 1996, Green filed a motion in federal district court asking
the court to enforce the final consent decree and to declare Horseshoe's
development of Riverwoods in violation of it.

Because Horseshoe and its partners had not yet received approval for
their development plan from the St. Louis County Council, which the
investors had petitioned in June 1995, Judge George Gunn, on February
28, sustained the Horseshoe Casino's motion to dismiss on grounds that
the case was not yet ripe for review.

But exactly a month later, the St. Louis County Council enacted an
ordinance approving the riverboat development (and describing it as
"essential to preserve and promote the public heath, safety and general

welfare of St. Louis County.")

Subsequently, on May 30, 1996, Harbor Venture attorney Martin Green filed in St. Louis County circuit court seeking a declaratory judgment that "the improvements and activities planned for the area are not prohibited by the restrictive covenants."

In fact, the petition to the court argued that the people walkway, service road and dock were expressly permitted by those covenants provision for the barge. As for the riverboat casino, it didn't come under governance of the covenants since it was on water, not land. And the Coalition shouldn't sue anyway because in 1976, when the Consent Decree and Earth City settlement were signed, the Coalition had agreed never to initiate new litigation on the issues.

Of course that powerful final persuader got a lot of emphasis in the suit: "Literally, millions of dollars are affected by this controversy, not only for Owner but also for St. Louis County. . . . Owners will be deprived of the opportunity to earn tens of millions of dollars and St. Louis County will be deprived of the opportunity to benefit from a project that will provide the County more than $100,000,000 during its first ten years of operation."

Following up on Judge Gunn's decision that the Coalition could refile its suit when the case was ripe for review, Green petitioned the federal court for transfer of the case filed by Harbor Venture in circuit court.

The case was removed to the court of Judge Stephen N. Limbaugh, Sr., on June 20, 1996. In August, Harbor Venture asked Limbaugh to send the case back to state circuit court, where the odds definitely were better for them. Limbaugh ruled against that idea. Donald Schupak and Jack Binion quit trying to make nice and changed lawyers. Martin Green of Green, Schaaf and Margo resigned. In his place, Harbor Venture hired Bryan Cave attorneys John "Jack" Danforth and Veryl Riddle, old friends of Judge Limbaugh.

Limbaugh, born in Cape Girardeau, owed Danforth his consideration for the bench. As a Republican senator for Missouri, Danforth, in 1983, nominated Limbaugh to President Ronald Reagan for appointment to a federal judgeship.

As for Veryl Riddle, he was a contemporary of Limbaugh from the same geographical and cultural territory. Both were natives of southeast

Missouri, growing up in the 1930s and 1940s when, Limbaugh noted, "there wasn't much attention paid to the environmental movement." Both were graduates of the University of Missouri at Columbia and Limbaugh, like Riddle, had been a litigator before his appointment.

Reached in November 2008, Limbaugh, now 81 and retired from the bench and working again as a litigator for the firm of Armstrong Teasdale, came across as careful how much he said, but plainspoken and sure of his convictions.

"There must have been a lot of pressure on you trying that case?" I offered.

"There was," he said simply, declining to elaborate.

Later in the conversation, he mentioned, "Jack Danforth recommended me (for the bench). They were all close associates. I liked them all."

Parsing a Barge?

Once again as he had in state court, Green argued the intent of a document dedicating land for public use. Once again he asserted that the primary mandate of the agreement was preservation of the land in its natural state and thus Harbor Venture's development was "expressly prohibited."

Attorneys Riddle and Danforth argued exactly the opposite: The riverboat terminal facility and the walkway were "expressly permitted" by the clause in the decree permitting barge mooring and loading and unloading of construction materials. The whole project designed to meet exactly the restrictions of the Consent Decree.

They produced a bunch of experts to testify on just what the term "barge" encompassed—how much square footage and what type of cargo.

And since they were arguing in front of a judge raised in Missouri's Republican outstate where an individual's right to do what he wanted with his land was sacred, they pointed out that Missouri law required restrictions on land use to be interpreted narrowly. "The Decree must be interpreted narrowly with an eye to the law that determines the landowner's rights, particularly where the restriction is purported to burden the property in perpetuity." In summary, they concluded they had every right to build a project on their own land.

On March 4, 1997, Judge Limbaugh handed up his order, which he emphasized he had arrived at after considering the meaning drawn from "the four corners of the Consent Decree," not the bias of Missouri property laws brought up in outside argument:

> *Having considered the entire consent order, the circumstances surrounding its formation and the list of prohibited uses expressly mentioned therein, the Court concludes that the parties never intended the term 'barge terminal facility' to encompass the passenger landing facility proposed by the Plaintiffs. Nor did they intend the phrase "appropriate facilities for the purpose of moving any gaseous, liquid or solid materials" to encompass an elevated walkway to assist riverboat casino passengers traveling across the area. . . . Accordingly the Court concludes that the Plaintiffs' intended use of the specified area . . . violates the terms of the consent order in Coalition for the Environment v. Volpe.*

The *Post-Dispatch* headline the next day read: "Ruling Threatens Casino Proposal."

Kathleen Henry, Lew Green's daughter, who now runs Great Rivers, the public interest law firm her father established, was working with him on the Harbor Venture case. "I remember how glad we were that Judge Limbaugh ruled in our favor even though Danforth was arguing for the other side," she recalled recently.

Mused Limbaugh, "You grow up influenced by a lot of things: family, schooling, politics, contacts. But you like to think you can make up your own mind anyway. I think I did. I like to think I made the proper decision on the points of law no matter what else was happening."

No one can recollect Lew Green's reaction to Limbaugh's ruling. He probably accepted it without hoopla since his personal victory had long been assured. He hadn't traded principle for cash. He stayed in league with the stones in the field.

For eight years after Judge Limbaugh's order preserving Riverwoods, it remained a tangle of deer trails and morning glory vines—and a management problem for the Conservation Department because of illegal dumping. Then, in 2005, the Great Rivers Greenway District, the public organization established by the voters in 2000 to lead the development of a regionwide system of interconnected parks and trails, proposed building a bicycle trail through Riverwoods. The city of Bridgeton, which held adjacent wetlands, enthusiastically endorsed the project and invited the Department of Conservation to give Bridgeton the park to maintain, a relinquishment the department was happy to permit.

The bike trail was completed in 2007, with fanfare and a ribbon-cutting.

"And that trail has been a blessing for us and Riverwoods because we have people down there all the time and there's no more dumping," said Walt Siemsglusz, the city's director of parks and recreation.

Both the Greenway District staff and Bridgeton personnel regard the strip of wetlands as a treasure.

"It's a destination park," said Siemsglusz. "It's one of the few places where people can actually get right down to the river, plus there are wonderful overlooks where you can see all of St. Charles. We've put some picnic tables down there. I never met Mr. Green, but I imagine this place turned out just the way he wanted."

CHAPTER 9

LAWSUIT TO ENFORCE
CLEAN AIR LAWS CAPS GREEN'S
CAREER-LONG CONCERN

Patricia Tummons

FOR LEWIS GREEN, THE LAWSUIT BROUGHT AGAINST THE ENVIRONMENTAL Protection Agency in November 1998 had to have been deeply personal. Thirty-three years earlier, then-Governor Warren E. Hearnes had appointed Green to be the first director of the newly minted Missouri Air Conservation Commission. Green took the charge seriously and worked tirelessly, at considerable personal cost, to develop a regulatory regime that would clear the state's air, particularly in the St. Louis region.

Testimony that Green provided to a subcommittee of the U.S. Senate shortly after he stepped down from that position showed his commitment to the cause and his prescient understanding of its dangers. The panel was holding hearings in St. Louis in September 1969, after a summer that had seen St. Louis shrouded for four days in a noxious, sulfurous cloud of smog.

"For nearly four years I have worked within the framework of the currently fashionable concepts of air pollution control in an effort to accelerate the urgently needed cleaning of our air in St. Louis," Green testified. "As the result of that experience, I have concluded that we will not make satisfactory progress until the federal government, and particularly the U.S. Congress, drastically revises certainly fundamental concepts now prevalent. . . .

"Air pollution is a national problem, and a hemispheric problem, and indeed a global problem. For example, for many years, the excessive carbon dioxide dumped into the Earth's atmosphere appeared in such quantities and for such duration that it caused the entire temperature of the Earth to rise steadily. The consequences of such a trend, in terms of melting glaciers and other phenomena, can be foreseen only dimly."

A few years later, Congress passed, and President Nixon signed, the Clean Air Act, with its promise of addressing on a national scale the very sort of pollutants Green had mentioned in his testimony.

Nearly three decades later, however, the air in St. Louis was continuing to fall short of standards set in the act. The low-hanging fruit in pollution control had been plucked; smokestack industries and other major polluters had been forced to take some measures to curb their emissions, but still the region's air did not meet national standards, especially when hot summer air moved in. The Missouri Legislature stubbornly refused to require reformulated gasoline and had only recently called for stepped-up vehicle emission inspections, measures that other states had taken to improve air quality.

Despite this, St. Louis had escaped penalties. The Environmental Protection Agency, charged by Congress with enforcing a series of deadlines for compliance, was turning out to be a toothless watchdog. By 1998, two years after the St. Louis area was to have met the standard for ozone, the EPA had not yet imposed mandated sanctions, which included reclassifying St. Louis as an area of "serious" non-attainment (from "moderate" non-attainment). This "bump-up," as it was called, could result in the loss of federal funds for new highway projects, among other things.

Under the Clean Air Act, the EPA was to have published a notice of its finding of non-attainment by May 15, 1997. Yet it had not done so by May 1998, when the Missouri Coalition for the Environment and the Sierra Club put the EPA on notice that the groups were intending to sue the agency under the citizen-suit provision of the Clean Air Act. On November 9, they made good on that threat, with Green, assisted by Saint Louis University Law School's Douglas Williams, filing a complaint on behalf of the two groups against the EPA, alleging numerous violations of the act.

AN ULTERIOR MOTIVE?

FOR SOME, THE TIMING OF THE LAWSUIT RAISED EYEBROWS. IT WAS FILED IN THE U.S. District Court for the District of Columbia on November 9, just six days after St. Louis–area voters had rejected a referendum measure that would have killed a controversial highway project known as the Page Avenue Extension. The road to link northern St. Louis and St. Charles counties had been in the planning stages for years, but opposition to it had grown. That summer, environmentalists had launched an initiative petition to put the matter before voters. Among other things, they argued that the road would encourage sprawl, burden the counties with additional costs of schools, sewers, and still more roads, and push population centers further west, thereby inflicting further damage on the St. Louis urban core.

Were the two groups whose members pushed for the petition seeking in the lawsuit to achieve what had been denied them by the voters? One of the sanctions that the EPA could impose, if the lawsuit was successful, was a cutoff of federal highway funds for new projects such as the Page Avenue Extension. Many members of the St. Louis–area business community as well as politicians were openly skeptical about motives for the complaint. On November 14, an editorial in the *St. Louis Post-Dispatch* gave voice to the skeptics, describing the lawsuit as "a tactic to continue the battle against Page Avenue."

The two groups objected to that characterization, which tended to mask the serious allegations contained in the lawsuit itself. In an op-ed piece that appeared in the *Post-Dispatch* on November 23, Roger Pryor of the Coalition and Ken Midkiff of the Sierra Club defended the legal action. "St. Louisans should make no mistake," they wrote. "This legal step was taken after very careful consideration of many factors, including the persistent, unhealthful smog that envelops St. Louis in summer. Our lawsuit is not suggesting that the U.S. Environmental Protection Agency should merely be tougher on St. Louis. Under the Clean Air Act Amendments of 1990, the EPA has no choice but to invoke sanctions. Sanctions are not discretionary."

A few months later, the *Post-Dispatch* again provided a forum for the view that the lawsuit was motivated by environmentalists disgruntled over the outcome of the November vote. In an article on February 19, reporter Tom Uhlenbrock quoted Richard Fleming, president of the St. Louis Regional Commerce and Growth Association, as saying the lawsuit was a case of sour grapes. "The timing of this lawsuit is curious at best," Fleming is reported to have said.

Pryor once more tried to quell the suspicion. A cut in highway funds "might delay" but would not stop construction of the Page Avenue Extension, he said, adding, "We announced this suit long before the Page vote took place. . . . I wish there was something that could knock Page off its pilings, but this is an issue about health in St. Louis."

A GAMBLE

ALMOST AS SOON AS THE COMPLAINT WAS FILED, ATTORNEYS FOR THE EPA AND THE Justice Department made an informal settlement proposal. In return for the Sierra Club and the Coalition dropping the lawsuit, the EPA would agree by August 2000 to act on (by approving or disapproving) four state implementation plans that Missouri would be required to submit for attaining air quality standards. (Missouri was required to submit them in any event, but had not yet done so.)

In a memo to his clients, Green set forth the pros and cons of the deal. "EPA claimed that this would be something specific, in hand, that we could enforce," Green wrote. "Maybe. But if we have a mild summer in 1999, or even 2000, EPA will declare that the St. Louis AQCR [Air Quality Control Region] has attained the [air quality standards]. . . . No court will compel EPA to compel Missouri to perform rituals designed to attain a standard which has already been attained, and is no longer applicable anyway. From any point of view, the consent decree appears to legitimize Missouri's past failures, simply establishing new deadlines, without any consequences for the past."

"EPA and Missouri have something to lose in the event of a hot summer. The settlement is designed to eliminate that risk for them," he wrote. "The question is: do we want to gamble?"

The offer was rejected.

MORE TIME

THE COMPLAINT, FILED IN THE U.S. DISTRICT COURT FOR THE DISTRICT OF Columbia, alleged that the EPA had ignored its duties under the Clean Air Act Amendments of 1990 by not imposing on the St. Louis area legally mandated consequences. The lawsuit listed seven separate breaches of duty, having to do with Missouri's failure to attain air quality standards and its submission of implementation plans for achieving those standards that fell short of the mark. The judge hearing the case, Colleen Kollar-Kotelly, was also asked to find that all determinations of conformity with respect to the area's federally approved transportation plans be set aside as invalid. The conformity determinations—findings that highway projects conform to the state's implementation plans (i.e., that they do not lead to reduced air quality)—were needed before any federal funds could be used on a project.

The EPA's special treatment of St. Louis had drawn attention of civic leaders and politicians in other non-attainment areas that had faced EPA-imposed sanctions. In a March 1999 memo to the court, concerning ozone levels in the St. Louis area, Green pointed out that although the EPA had notified Missouri's governor that the state's efforts to solve the air quality problem were not sufficient, the EPA "continues to search for ways to avoid performing the clear mandate of the statute. . . . This separate and individualized regulatory treatment has not gone unnoticed by other similarly situated [Air Quality Control Regions], each of which has been subject to regulatory standards that have not been applied to the St. Louis AQCR. . . . In response to concerns that the Dallas-Fort Worth area was not receiving the same regulatory treatment as other moderate areas, particularly the St. Louis area, EPA provided a detailed explanation of how it was implementing the Clean Air Act in moderate non-attainment areas and how these actions conformed to the Clean Air Act. When it got to St. Louis, however, the agency could muster no explanation at all for its failure to 'bump up' the AQCR."

The "apparently inconsistent positions," Green argued, "have generated concerns in Congress and among other states that EPA is giving the St. Louis area some sort of unexplained special treatment."

The EPA responded to the lawsuit by challenging the adequacy of the plaintiffs' notice of intent to sue, arguing that because the letters giving notice did not provide exhaustive chapter-and-verse citations of the EPA's alleged shortcomings, five of the counts should be tossed out of court, while one was untimely. And if the court wasn't buying that, the EPA argued that the law did not authorize the courts to order the remedies sought by the plaintiffs.

(In an effort to cure any deficiencies in the notice letters, Green hastily filed another notice of intent to sue in December 1998, and in January 1999, without waiting for the 60-day notice period to expire, filed a second lawsuit, virtually identical to the first. The tactic failed: in January 2000, Judge Kollar-Kotelly threw out the second lawsuit, as well as the counts in the first lawsuit that the EPA had argued were not sufficiently detailed in the notice letters or were unripe for litigation.)

As if to moot the sole count that the EPA acknowledged might have validity—its failure to determine that St. Louis was a non-attainment area for ozone—in March 1999, the agency published in the *Federal Register* a notice that it was *proposing* to find that St. Louis had missed the November 1996 deadline for achieving the ozone standard, but that it would hold off on *finalizing* the determination. This delay would give Missouri and Illinois until November 15, 1999, to show that they should qualify for a time extension as a result of air quality in the region being affected by pollution sources outside the area, under a policy that the EPA had developed on its own that called for giving downwind areas more time than the Clean Air Act called for to attain national standards. Only if the two states failed to make a showing to the EPA that they qualified for the special treatment the agency was affording to downwind areas would the agency then "finalize" its finding of St. Louis's failure to attain, with the area then being reclassified to one of "serious" non-attainment. If the EPA did qualify the area for consideration as a region where air quality was affected by upwind pollution, then the deadline for attaining air quality standards would coincide with the date set for reducing the upwind pollution—in 2003, the *Federal Register* notice stated.

Green did not hide his contempt for the EPA's proposal. In a footnote to a filing with the court, he wrote: "Under the guise of proposing a remedy for its admitted failure to perform the nondiscretionary duties alleged in Count I, EPA is seeking surreptitiously to end this litigation without ever addressing the merits of plaintiffs' legal challenges."

"EPA's main concern in this litigation is to avoid having the St. Louis area 'bumped up' to the status of a serious ozone non-attainment area," Green told the court. "That is the *only* reason EPA has failed formally to set forth its determination in a *Federal Register* notice as required by" the Clean Air Act.

Over the next two years, the court was buffeted by motions and countermotions from Green and Williams and their adversaries in the federal government. By January 2001, two issues remained for the judge to decide. First to be disposed of was the accusation that the EPA had failed to approve or disapprove Missouri's proposed state implementation plan (SIP) within the time required by the Clean Air Act. In May 2000, however, the EPA published notice that it had approved a revised SIP for Missouri. The EPA argued, and the judge agreed, that this made the complaint moot. And while the plaintiffs may have asked the judge to rule on the sufficiency of the SIP, she agreed with the EPA that the Clean Air Act called for any challenge to the approved plan to be filed in the federal appeals court covering the region.

With that disposed of, the sole remaining issue before the judge was whether the EPA had violated the Clean Air Act by failing to publish a finding that the St. Louis area was in serious noncompliance with the ozone standard.

On this point, the plaintiffs prevailed. Although the judge did not issue the finding of non-attainment herself, she did order the EPA to publish notice of its final determination by March 12 (a deadline that was later, for practical reasons, extended to March 19).

"ANIMOSITY AND CHAGRIN"

THE ENVIRONMENTAL PROTECTION AGENCY HAD ASKED THE COURT IF IT COULD delay publication of the non-attainment notice until June 29, 2001, "and possibly until June 22, 2002," before issuing the determination that was supposed to have been published no later than May 15, 1997. The EPA argued that the extension was warranted, since, in separate litigation, the Federal District Court for the District of Columbia had given the agency permission to extend the time allowed—until at least May 31,

2004—for areas of upwind pollution to control emissions that contributed to downwind areas' non-attainment.

The judge rejected the request: "Nothing in the statute affords the court any flexibility with regard to developing an alternative timing schedule that bends along with a state's efforts and EPA's reactions thereto," the judge wrote. "In fact, allowing for the flexible schedule with alternative deadlines that EPA proposes would effectively amount to condoning a fully discretionary approach to a non-discretionary duty. . . . The statutory duty is not simply to 'determine' and 'publish' in the abstract. It is to 'determine' and 'publish' by date certain."

The reaction to the judge's decision among business groups in the St. Louis area was surprisingly mild, suggesting that it had been informed already of the EPA's strategy to address the ruling. Norb Plassmeyer, a mouthpiece for the group Associated Industries of Missouri (which had been granted intervenor standing in the lawsuit), told the group's members in March 2001 that "a plan by US EPA and endorsed by AIM would allow the area to continue on its current path . . . without being reclassified as 'serious' non-attainment. In essence, EPA plans to extend the 'effective date' for an attainment determination until June 29, 2001. . . . The determination is significant because it provides an alternative plan to the ruling sought by the Sierra Club of Missouri and the Missouri Coalition for the Environment."

The director of the state's Air Conservation Commission was not so blasé, suggesting he was not privy to the same information EPA had given to AIM. In a report that AIM published of the February meeting of the commission, the commission's director, Roger Randolph, was quoted as telling commission members that if the St. Louis area were "bumped up" to the status of serious non-attainment, "we would be very disappointed. . . . That is the polite way for me to say it. Mixed company does not allow me to express my animosity and chagrin" at the judgment.

THE NEXT LEVEL

RANDOLPH'S FEARS WERE UNFOUNDED, AS PLASSMEYER KNEW THEY WERE. ON March 19, the *Federal Register* included the EPA's determination that the St. Louis area had, indeed, failed to attain the ozone standard by the November 1996 deadline. However, despite earlier contentions by the EPA that the effective date of such determinations was the date notice published, now it was announcing that the effective date and the bumped-up reclassification of St. Louis to a "serious" non-attainment area would be put off for 60 days, until June 29, 2001. The EPA made its proposed finding final on May 16.

But on June 26, the EPA granted the St. Louis area a time extension for attaining air quality standards, invoking its downwind extension policy. At the same time, it withdrew its earlier non-attainment finding and the reclassification of St. Louis into the status of a "serious" non-attainment area.

In July 2001, Green and Williams filed a motion with Judge Kollar-Kotelly, asking her to enforce her order. "On its own initiative," they wrote, "EPA has chosen to give itself the discretion this court held was inconsistent with the Clean Air Act.... This court should not permit EPA to achieve a result that this court concluded was unlawful and prohibited by a clear statutory mandate.... EPA has simply—and baldly—defied the clear import of this court's order."

Efforts to get Judge Kollar-Kotelly to remedy the perceived shortcomings in the EPA actions were quickly dropped. Instead, the plaintiffs turned their attention to the U.S. Court of Appeals for the 7th Circuit, where on July 13, they filed two appeals, one concerning the EPA's notice of May 16, and the second of its June 26 time extension. The two suits were consolidated, and the appeals court scheduled hearings on the arguments for April 15, 2002. (Judge Kollar-Kotelly's decision was appealed separately to the Court of Appeals for the District of Columbia Circuit. The decision in that case, essentially upholding the judge's ruling, was issued just 10 days before oral arguments were heard in the 7th Circuit.)

The appeal of the EPA's grant of a time extension to the St. Louis area drew a number of intervenors. Not only did the states of Missouri and Illinois weigh in, but also various business groups in the St. Louis area, the Regional Commerce and Growth Association, the Missouri Chamber of Commerce, the Associated Industries of Missouri, the Associated General Contractors of Missouri, the Associated General Contractors of St. Louis, and the Heavy Constructors Association of Greater Kansas City. Georgia and Louisiana filed a joint *amicus* brief, stating that they had a stake in the outcome of the court's evaluation of the EPA's policy to grant time extensions to areas affected by upwind pollution.

As suggested in the list of intervenors, EPA policies were being challenged in areas other than St. Louis. In Atlanta, the EPA was being sued by the Southern Organizing Committee for Economic and Social Justice and the Sierra Club over the agency's foot-dragging in determining Atlanta to be in serious non-attainment of clean air standards. And in the Court of Appeals for the District of Columbia Circuit, the Sierra Club was challenging the EPA's approval of revised implementation plans for achieving ozone standards in the Washington, D.C., metropolitan area. (Both Missouri and Illinois had intervened in this case as well.) Other challenges to EPA policies were being pursued in San Francisco, Sacramento, and Houston.

SHORT-LIVED RELIEF

FOR MORE THAN SEVEN MONTHS AFTER ORAL ARGUMENTS WERE HEARD, THE THREE-judge panel of the 7th Circuit kept Green, Williams, and the plaintiffs waiting. Finally, on November 25, 2002, the court published its decision, soundly vindicating Green's position.

The court found nothing in the Clean Air Act supported the EPA's protracted delays in finding the St. Louis area to be in "serious" non-attainment status. While under some circumstances the law allows EPA to grant "no more than 2 one-year extensions" of the attainment deadline, the court wrote, the EPA's actions in response to the Sierra Club and Coalition lawsuit had extended St. Louis's attainment deadline by eight years. "Because we find that the EPA has no authority to create such an extension, we . . . order the agency to redesignate St. Louis a serious non-attainment area," wrote Circuit Judge Diane Wood.

The EPA had argued that Congress was unaware of transported pollution and never intended to impose punishment on areas that bore this burden. "The statute itself reveals that the EPA's theory that Congress was unaware of transported pollution is mistaken," Judge Wood wrote. In several sections, she noted, Congress did address the problem of transport, although the solution it devised "was not as sweeping as the EPA now would like."

"Indeed," Wood wrote, "we take issue with the EPA's most basic premise: that the CAA harbors within its structure a broad intent never to impose penalties on states burdened by transport." Congress, she continued, "did not want to wait around for the EPA to determine how much, if any, of an area's pollution was the result of transport and how much was home-grown. . . . It also specified concrete deadlines and mandated that areas failing to meet those deadlines 'shall be reclassified.' Faced with such clear language, we find that Congress did not delegate to the EPA any authority to grant extensions of more than two years based on interstate transport."

The court, finding that the EPA's extension policy is "contrary to the unambiguous text" of the Clean Air Act, vacated the time extension granted to St. Louis in the EPA's June 26, 2001, rule and remanded the matter back to the EPA "for entry of a final rule that reclassifies St. Louis as a serious non-attainment area effective immediately."

In January 2003, the EPA published what has to be one of the most confusing rules ever gracing the pages of the *Federal Register*. On the one hand, complying with the court's order, it found St. Louis to be an area of serious non-attainment. On the other, it determined that, based on St. Louis having attained compliance with the ozone standard in 2002, the area was to be considered an attainment area.

As the Missouri Department of Natural Resources described the situation in its annual report, "the proposal to redesignate the area to attainment and the final rule reclassifying the area to serious were published simultaneously in the *Federal Register*." On May 12, 2003, four days before Green's death, the EPA published a final determination that St. Louis had been redesignated as an attainment area for ozone.

But the relief was not to last long. In 2004, a new ozone standard took effect, and once more, St. Louis faced an uphill battle to meet it. From the one-hour ozone standard (0.12 parts per million not to be exceeded for one hour), EPA shifted to a more stringent eight-hour standard (0.08 ppm average ozone concentration over eight hours). Although the EPA had adopted the change in 1997, because of court challenges, the new standard did not become effective until June 2004. St. Louis's attainment of the ozone standard could apparently be achieved only so long as it could be held to an outdated goal. In 2008, when the EPA ozone standard was made even more stringent, at 0.075 ppm averaged over eight hours, St. Louis–area air quality monitors reported exceedances 19 times on eight separate days.

Appendix A

Milestones in the Life of Lewis Cox Green, 1924–2003

October 14, 1924: Lewis Cox Green is born in St. Louis to John Raeburn Green and Elisabeth Haskell Cox Green.

1941: Graduates from Country Day School, St. Louis County, where he receives the Latin Prize.

1942-46: Serves in the U.S. Army Signal Corps.

1947: Graduates from Harvard University.

1950: Graduates *magna cum laude* from Harvard Law School, where he was an editor of the *Harvard Law Review*.

1950-51: Law clerk to Judge William E. Orr, U.S. Court of Appeals for the 9th Circuit.

1951-52: Law Clerk to Justice Stanley F. Reed, Supreme Court of the United States.

1952-54: Works in the Appellate Division of the Office of General Counsel, National Labor Relations Board.

1954: Marries Louise Stewart Goold and returns to the St. Louis area. Becomes active in Democratic Party politics.

1955-56: Law Clerk to Judge George H. Moore, U.S. District Judge.

1958: Is elected Democratic Committeeman, Bonhomme Township.

1958-1975: Democratic Committeeman, Bonhomme Township.

1962: Runs unsuccessfully for state representative against Republican incumbent Robert Snyder. Is endorsed by the *St. Louis Post-Dispatch* as a "lawyer of exceptional ability who . . . has the potential to become the county delegation's outstanding member if elected."

1965-69: First Chairman of the Air Conservation Commission of Missouri.

1968: Formation of the Missouri Coalition for the Environment, an outgrowth of the Open Space Council and the Committee for Environmental Information. Green is one of the founding members, along with Leo Drey, John Brawley, Virginia Brodine, and Barry Commoner.

1970: Is named "Air Conservationist of the Year" by the Conservation Federation of Missouri and the National Wildlife Federation.

1971: Receives the Newspaper Guild Page One Civic Award. Among other things, the award noted: "During Mr. Green's tenure as Democratic Committeeman of Bonhomme Township he successfully pushed to have air pollution control on the party's gubernatorial platform. This campaign pledge resulted in the passage of the state's first air pollution control law."

1975-1979: Attorney for the city of Bridgeton, Missouri.

1978: Receives the Environmental Quality Award from the U.S. Environmental Protection Agency.

1979: Receives Environmental Activist Award from the Missouri Coalition for the Environment.

1993: The Sierra Club awards Life Member standing to Mr. and Mrs. Lewis C. Green, "in recognition of a lifetime commitment to the preservation of wilderness and the goals of the Sierra Club."

1994: Receives the "Silver Steward Award" from the Coalition for the Environment for more than a quarter century of outstanding environmental service.

1998: The Missouri Association for Social Welfare, St. Louis Chapter, honors Green as "Advocate of the year" for "persistently working to achieve social justice for all Missourians, including low income citizens."

1999: After 13 years, Green's litigation against the Metropolitan St. Louis Sewer District for violations of Missouri's "Hancock Amendment," limiting fee increases, is concluded, with MSD agreeing to pay a settlement of $40 million for overcharges. Fifteen percent of that is to go for attorneys' fees and costs.

2002: Establishes the Great Rivers Environmental Law Center, a non-profit law firm, to continue his legacy of public interest environmental litigation.

May 16, 2003: Death.

Appendix B

Tributes in Honor of Lewis Cox Green

LEWIS GREEN'S ACHIEVEMENTS AND INTERESTS WERE NOT LIMITED TO THE FIELD of environmental litigation. As the tributes and reminiscences of friends and colleagues presented here attest, his interests were catholic and his talents no less diverse.

VINCENT McKUSICK

McKusick is a former Chief Justice of the Maine Supreme Court.

LEW AND I WERE VERY CLOSELY ASSOCIATED IN TWO PERIODS IN OUR INTRODUCTORY days in the law—three years at Harvard Law School in the Class of 1950, with two of those years (1948–50) spent as hardworking colleagues on the Board of Editors of the *Harvard Law Review* and then one year in the October Term 1951 of the Supreme Court of the United States (August 1951 through July 1952) as law clerks to two of the Justices.

On the *Review,* which I headed during our third year, Lew was a tower of strength and a much liked associate in the hard work required to publish the *Review.* That year the *Review,* as the result of a self study of its operations during the previous year, instituted a number of new features, which included: the "comment," a shorter form of lead article written by outside authors; the "Supreme Court Note," a full-scale student analysis (appearing in each November issue) of the Supreme Court decisions of the preceding term; and the "Developments in the Law" (appearing fairly late in each *Review* year), exploring at length a selected legal subject. Lew was in charge of the third of these innovations; he was the first Developments Editor of the *Review.* Lew was critical to the highly successful launching of this new feature. The *Review* continued publishing the "Developments in the Law" established by Lew for a good many years. It is interesting to note that the *Review* at its current internet web site still offers reprints of past Developments in the Law. Lew in the midst of working very hard in class and on the *Law Review* always had an easy-going way about him and a fine sense of humor of his very own variety. He was a wonderful member of the *Review* brotherhood—yes, indeed, a brotherhood because Volume 63 [1950] was the last volume of the *Review* published before women were admitted to Harvard Law School.

After graduating from law school in June 1950, Lew and I went off to clerk for U.S. Appeals Court judges in different circuits, he in the 9th Circuit and I in the 2nd, but happy fate in 1951–52 brought us back together again to clerk at the Supreme Court, Lew for Justice Stanley F. Reed and I for Justice Felix Frankfurter. Again, Lew and I worked very hard in serving our judicial bosses, but we had a good deal of opportunity to get together at the Court and outside. FF, as "my" justice was familiarly called, at least subsequently to clerking for him, was a great "Pied Piper of Hamelin," attracting clerks from other chambers for what seemed at times like a graduate law seminar. FF from his Harvard Law School teaching days and beyond knew Lew's father (who was in the Class of 1917 and had a very distinguished career—starting with service on the *Harvard Law Review*) and so Lew was especially welcome in the Frankfurter chambers.

I have heard much about John Raeburn Green. Lew without making a big deal of it always quietly showed his great respect for his father. Although I do not remember having met the father, it is clear to me that the son acquired and nurtured the father's sense of what is right and wrong and his high standard of conduct and integrity. I know that makes Lew sound pompous and self-righteous. Lew was not at all that. He had a self-effacing and sometimes self-deprecating sense of humor, as well as a way of speaking that put all at ease. On the other hand, he was never bashful about stating his mind. Typical of Lew's no-nonsense approach is his 1965 response to the usual request for personal biographical information and comments for the 15th Year Class Report: He said only: "Too busy to sound off."

After Washington our careers took Lew and me in different geographical directions. Nonetheless Louise and Lew remained in contact with Nancy and Vincent through a regular exchange of Christmas greetings and report, through Lew's and my joint service for a time in the

National Conference of Commissioners on Uniform State Laws, and through regular Harvard Law School Reunions. I count myself fortunate to have had the friendship of Lewis C. Green for 57 years.

Kay Drey

Drey and her husband, Leo, were close friends of Louise and Lewis Green. Green represented both of them in lawsuits and appeals too numerous to mention.

Because of Lew Green, we have cleaner air and water, and some of the world's best remaining flood plains and parks. And environmental laws. Lew fought against Sewer District shenanigans, and against nuclear power, and against plutonium at Mizzou, and weapons of mass destruction at Fort Leonard Wood. He was, of course, fighting *for* our environment.

As Leo keeps saying to me, Lew made a huge difference. A *huge* difference. He was very demanding of government, his family and friends, *and* of himself. Even as he got older, he worked long hours—all night, if necessary. His briefs were masterpieces of persuasion, careful research, and logic, with hidden sparks of humor. I sometimes wondered why he didn't get disbarred because of the strong things he said about judges who had made mistakes, or about county supervisors. His briefs all seemed correct to me, and breathtakingly brilliant.

Lew was tough and demanding, but underneath or above all that, he could be gentle, sensitive, and appreciative. He loved his wonderful family, and his associates and friends, and dogs—*everyone's* dogs. And we *all* loved Lew, in return.

Jim Wilson

Wilson is a former city counselor for the city of St. Louis and is a partner in the law firm of Berg, Borgmann, Wilson, & Wolk. He serves as chairman of the board of directors of the Great Rivers Environmental Law Center.

I was asked to speak as the chairman of the Great Rivers board of directors, a co-counsel, and also an adversary of Lewis. And I was asked to keep it short.

I could get off easy and talk about Lewis and simply say he loved the law. And he was very educated and as Lewis would say he loved the law and I won't use the word workaholic, but he puts someone like myself to shame. He was considered by many the consummate professional.

He took on cases that had very little chance of success, for no remuneration. But he took them on. And he took them on against forces that had much more resources, manpower, and financial whatever, and the odds of success were very, very slight. But I think he felt, as an advocate, if he did not take those causes on he would not have been worth much as a professional. The bottom line I think for Lew was that the measure of an attorney is not what he receives from the public or society but what he can contribute to society.

I could probably stop there, but I'm going to go one step further. I think I know the particular mission of Lew. And that was to hold government responsible and to require government to obey the law just as it requires its citizens.

I first met Lewis about 25 years ago. I happened to be arguing a case before the Missouri Supreme Court and he was in one of his major battles with a governmental entity and his reputation was there at the time as a very distinguished public interest lawyer.

A few years later I encountered him as an adversary when he took on the city of St. Louis, and as a government attorney defending the usual skullduggery of government, I would have to say I always tried to do the right thing, but it was sometimes a matter of avoidance of the law, not violating the law.

Oftentimes lawyers develop the most respect for each other not necessarily as lawyers on the same side but as adversaries, and I developed a great deal of respect for Lew. I think his particular point was that if government did not follow or adhere to the laws, how could it expect its citizenry to do so.

I think Lew saw any disrespect for the law as a violation of societal interests. In a way, he was a great defender of our legal system, I think unwittingly. I would describe him as a conservative. Lew, please forgive me for using the "C" word. I think that was his point—that the legal system needed to be preserved and if government crossed the line he would attempt to make it tow the line with the means that he had available, which was litigation.

Last comment, if you mention in legal circles, in the city of St. Louis, 'public interest lawyer,' one name and one name only would probably pop up: Lewis Green. It is a vanishing breed. Most lawyers will do pro bono work representing specific individuals. The public interest lawyer represents a broad swath of citizenry. Today there are walking the streets of this region a lot of citizens who benefited by Lewis's work because of the many causes he participated in. They will never know Lewis nor have even heard of him. That, I guess, is the irony of being a public interest lawyer.

BRUCE MORRISON

Morrison is general counsel with the Great Rivers Environmental Law Center. Before that, he worked closely with Green in the firm Green, Hennings & Henry.

IN THE SUMMER OF 1988 I HAD BEEN WITH THE FIRM FOR THREE WEEKS. LEWIS took me to the chambers of Judge Clyde Cahill. Five lawyers against Lewis. And he was amazing. As we were leaving, the judge's law clerk said to me, "Wow, your Mr. Green is really something." What a wonderful teacher I was to have.

Lewis could view a case from a perspective no other lawyer would think of. He would tell me that he was "no good with people," that his thing "was analyzing documents." Still, he would study the judges in our cases, always taking that extra step. For one appeal, we learned that the judge was a Civil War historian. We spent some time brushing up on our history on the chance that a Civil War reference or two in our brief would tilt the scales our way. We lost that one, but not on account of anything we wrote. Simply, the judge "was no damn good," as Lewis would say.

What a communicator Lewis could be. His writings were beautiful. He was a gifted speaker. Even with these gifts, though, he was capable of communicating as badly as the rest of us. From time to time I would find myself complaining to him, "you never told me that," with Lewis responding, "I'm sure I told you." After Lewis's third or fourth, "I'm sure I told you," the jousting would end with my asking him, "Well, was I listening?" Lewis would smile ever so slightly and say, "Apparently not."

He had high expectations of others. Sure, he could be critical; he could be gruff at times. Beneath that, though, was one kind, compassionate soul. When my father moved away, Lewis was stuck bridging the gap. We spent the next 14 years together from about 9 to 6, Monday through Friday, and some Saturdays, too. Most of the time we worked. Occasionally we played, taking in a ball game, with Lewis finding some incredibly worn cap to wear.

Our times together were not always stress-free. Twice, I found myself sobbing in his office, struggling with a personal loss. Talk about putting the man on the spot! Lewis was no Dr. Phil. He was not one to say, "Let it out, share your feelings." I never saw Lewis look as uncomfortable as he looked on those days.

Lewis took an interest in my life's good news as well. His daughter Katy reminds me that her dad insisted that I telephone the now love of my life. I don't know whether Lewis was genuinely interested in seeing that I had a date for the weekend, or whether he just couldn't bear to see me waste away the work day, trying to decide whether to telephone the woman.

He adored his grandchildren. His face would light up when they came to the office. And when my son would visit, Lewis would greet him with a hug, and send him off with another one.

And dogs, they could have the run of the place. Not long ago one client dropped in for a conference. As he reached for a cigarette, he told us that he had brought his dog, and that the dog was in the utility closet outside the office. We told the client that the dog was welcome but that the cigarette was not. For the duration of that cigarette break, the dog and the client traded places. I can still hear Lewis laughing as that big dog ran down the hall and into his office.

What a wonderful teacher I had.

JOE LOGAN

Logan, like Green, is a graduate of Harvard Law (1948). He and his wife, Yvonne, were close friends of the Greens. Logan is a partner in the St. Louis firm of Thompson Coburn.

I HAVE INDEED BEEN BLESSED IN MY LIFE IN MANY WAYS. CERTAINLY ONE OF THESE blessings has been the friendship of Lewis for many years. During this time we traveled together—with Kay and Leo Drey—to Costa Rica and Sicily. We floated together on the Current and Jack's Fork rivers in the Ozarks. We debated political and social issues in our Great Decisions group, and we met weekly for lunch on Wednesdays with a group of caring and articulate friends to argue, discuss, and speculate about what might happen in St. Louis, the country, and the world. I became well acquainted with Lewis and enjoyed his friendship very much.

Lewis was a true gentle-man. He never swore or told coarse jokes—or even listened to one being told if he could avoid it. He instinctively knew what were good manners and what was pretentious posturing. That's why he could get away with wearing those caps in the house even when he and Louise were entertaining.

Lewis was very intelligent and had a good memory. Unlike me. For example, I might attempt to describe to Lewis a recent court action I had read about. Then I would ask Lewis if he happened to have read about that recent ruling. He might think a moment and then say that he thought he did read about it but, if it is the ruling or event I had been thinking about, it had occurred in New Mexico and not Nebraska, or the court was not the state Supreme Court but rather the United States District Court, and the ruling was not a decision on the merits but in connection with a motion for a temporary injunction.

This happened a number of times and I sometimes worried about getting on Lewis's "dummies" list. There may be some connection between this and the fact that Lewis graduated from Harvard Law School *magna cum laude* and I managed to get a C average. I sometimes described a person to Lewis as being "almost as smart as you are."

At our Great Decisions meetings, I usually tried to avoid expressing my own opinion on the issue being discussed until I had heard from Lewis.

Lewis had a great sense of humor and one of the ways he indulged in this sometimes would be to tell wonderful anecdotes which were completely fictional—all with a straight face. One time there was something in the news about Mayor Freeman Bosley's father, the alderman, having a mattress manufacturing business in north St. Louis. I made some remark about this probably being a front for some nefarious activity. Lewis said, "Oh, no, I have bought mattresses from him. He isn't always in and sometimes I have had to wait on the street for him to come and open the door." This seemed preposterous to me and I told him so. But he stuck with his story. Maybe this is an example of the "bleak" humor that Florence Shinkle mentioned in her fine obituary carried in the *Post-Dispatch*.

Lewis sometimes was regarded as gruff and garrulous. Although he did not suffer fools gladly, he was, in fact, a softy with a particular fondness for small children and dogs. He never met a dog he did not like.

So, I believe that all of us here today share in the blessing of having had this wonderful man as a friend. In closing, I say to you all and to Louise, Rusty, Annie, Katy, and Mary . . . "oh, shoot!"

[Editor's note: Louise Green says Lewis was telling the truth. He sometimes bought mattresses from Mayor Bosley's father.]

PAT MARTIN

Martin, a community activist in St. Louis, was represented as plaintiff by Green in several lawsuits. She died in 2009.

I KNEW LEWIS AS A PATIENT, KIND, AND EXPERT TEACHER. WHO ELSE WOULD TAKE the time to thoroughly explain to a non-lawyer the nuances of the Equal Protection Clause of our federal and state constitutions? And then *make sure* (again and again) that this non-lawyer understood it!

I knew Lewis as a perfectionist—the very best kind—in his work. He always checked, and checked again, to make sure he got it right—whether it was a case citation or the grammar used in his writing. He wouldn't tolerate sloppiness and we who were involved with him in some of the battles he fought appreciated that and were inspired by it.

I knew Lewis as just a wonderful human being. He really cared about *people*. He gave himself, his talent, and his knowledge and wisdom so willingly. If it was about righting a wrong, or trying to prevent a wrong, you didn't need to ask to know where Lewis would be on the issue.

Lewis was involved all his life in battling injustice. Injustice on many, many different fronts. And he did it with extraordinary skill and insight, and extraordinary humility.

Lewis had exceptional courage in taking on politically unpopular causes. Whether it was corruption, ineptitude, deliberate misconduct, or any of the misdeeds or unlawful acts of government or corporations, he didn't hesitate. Lewis may be best known to the public for his important work on legal issues concerning environmental protections. But he was involved with many diverse issues, and I'm sure I don't know about even half of them. Some I do know are:

• Trying to get the new 1974 initiative campaign finance disclosure law correctly administered and enforced;

• Challenging the biased language presented to voters about ballot propositions;

• Challenging the constitutionality of the Hancock Amendment, both soon after it was passed in 1980, and later in 1997 and 1998;

• Helping to decipher the complex language in sales tax proposals, and helping to oppose them and other regressive tax measures;

• Challenging the Metropolitan St. Louis Sewer District's actions on many different issues;

• Drafting innumerable initiative petitions and legislation—but only after careful and exhaustive research;

• Helping citizens oppose corporate welfare—most recently on the use of public funds for the Cardinals' new baseball stadium, while the state and city and county don't have enough money to provide basic human services.

In short, Lewis was a unique human being, and he is simply irreplaceable.

Our lives and community will not be the same without Lewis. It is as if one of its strong supporting pillars has been removed. We will all need to work harder now, but we can be forever grateful for all he taught us, and for the inspiration he has given us. Because he so willingly shared his devotion to justice, I know he will still be part of our future efforts as we work for that goal.

John Arnold

Arnold is a St. Louis attorney and former law partner of Green's.

My first recollection of Lew was about 40 years ago, when, just released from active duty, I joined the law firm that bore the names of his grandfather and my father. I was in our law library when Lew, in shirt sleeves and stocking feet with his tie undone and a pencil in his teeth, shared with me his view of an 8th Circuit opinion which he was waving in my face. "Why, that silly old fool!" he said. Lew was not tolerant of judges or lawyers: he was tolerant of children and of dogs. I thoroughly enjoyed the half-dozen years in which we practiced together while he was engaged in the electrical and aluminum anti-trust cases and defamation lawsuits. Occasionally, when challenged on some obscure point, Lew would say: "I am waiting for someone smarter than I to figure that out." While I waited, he figured it out. He was a marvelous teacher with a wicked sense of humor.

Several years ago, novelist Richard North Patterson wrote: Americans hate every lawyer but their own—every lawsuit but the one they want to bring—just as they respect every law but the one they intend to break. Disparaging comments about lawyers are simply cover for community complicity. When social conscience dies, the law thrives.

Lew Green was our environmental social conscience long before it was fashionable. In 1964, he volunteered to write speeches on air and water pollution and open space for a challenger for the Democratic nomination for governor. When elected, Governor Warren Hearnes asked Lew to draft Missouri's air pollution law and to become the first chairman of our Air Conservation Commission. Lew spent a major portion of the next 35 years representing environmentalists—often without compensation—in claims under the National Environmental Policy Act to enforce air and water pollution laws and to protect open space and flood plains.

Lew was foremost a lawyer—one of those who smooth out difficulties, correct mistakes, take up the burdens of others, and strive to make possible a peaceful life in a peaceful state. He was a public interest lawyer as interested in campaign finance disclosure, ballot proposition language, and the constitutionality of debt limitations as he was in the environment. But it was the environment that occupied most of his energy. Because Lew was as demanding of government as he was of private industry, many of his environmental claims were filed against public agencies—the U.S. Army Corps of Engineers, the Missouri Highway Commission, the U.S. Secretary of Transportation, the Missouri Conservation Commission, the U.S. Department of Energy, the Environmental Protection Agency, and the Nuclear Regulatory Commission to ensure that these public agencies fulfilled their obligations to serve the public interest.

Last year, Lew established the Great Rivers Environmental Law Center, a not-for-profit, public interest law firm, to carry on the pro bono representation of environmental cases dealing with clean air and water and equity in the siting of environmental facilities.

Death is but a horizon: a horizon which limits only our sight. Lewis C. Green remains with us: our colleague in the law—with his invitation to join him—in the public interest.

Marvin Boisseau

Boisseau, who died in 2009, was a St. Louis judge and longtime lawyer and political figure in St. Louis Democratic circles.

I met Lew Green in law school where he was a year behind me. I had heard of him before from his older sister, a classmate in high school. She went on to become active in politics in North Carolina. Lew went on from the *Law Review* to clerking for the Supreme Court along with Rehnquist, among others, whom Lew described as very conservative even as a young man.

After work with the NLRB and marriage, Lew and his bride moved to University City—Hadley Township, where I'd been active in Democratic politics since I returned from Law School in '49. About this time we worked on a project for the Fund for the Republic instigated by Adam Yarmolinsky, another of Lew's colleague clerks with the Supreme Court.

I was appointed to the County Central Committee from Hadley in

'55, and Lew was also active in the '56 presidential campaign when Adlai Stevenson carried Missouri, despite the coming together of the Suez Crisis and the Hungarian revolt against the Soviets that helped re-elect Eisenhower. Lew and Louise Green had moved to Kirkwood and he got on the committee from Bonhomme Township either by appointment in '57 or election in '58.

The committeewoman there, Madeira Williams, I'd known for a number of years in church, and she and Lew made a good team. We worked hard for Kennedy in '60, when we carried him in St. Louis County and the state by 10,000 votes. We did infuse some life and energy in the committee and the party. Many of our predecessors just went through the motions in elections, relying on the Democratic vote in other parts of the state to keep them in their "license office" jobs—Department of Revenue.

After the '60 election Lew and I had some wheeling and dealing with the Post Office in connection with patronage, but I've forgotten the details. We did elect a new chairman of our committee after a long and interesting campaign and night meeting.

In the '60 primary for attorney general I did not care for Tom Eagleton's father having practically bought the circuit attorney's office for him in '56, but Lew was all for him, probably because he'd been *Harvard Law Review,* also. Because his more experienced opponent was in the 2nd or "obituary" column in our big voting machines, it was easy to endorse him. Lew was taken aback and I a little less so when Eagleton's bag man came around to each of us with three $100 bills for primary expenses.

After the '60 Primary we had an interesting campaign for chairman. Lew and I decided the only one we really could elect was Johnson from Concord Township. Bob Young wanted it, but he had only four votes. (He did get more years later, serving several terms in Congress and getting his name on a government building.) Sid McClanahan from Jefferson Township wanted a "man of stature." Lew, he, and I were all considerably taller than Johnson. We did prevail with the short man after several votes.

Probably our most noteworthy accomplishment was defeating the county supervisor in the '62 Primary. Lew and I were alone in starting that campaign, but we ultimately prevailed. Our nominee did run out of gas in the general.

Another Pyrrhic victory in the '62 Primary was instigated by Lew in behalf of a friend of his who was running for the still elective office of circuit judge. The endorsement of Lew's candidate by Johnson was needed, so I had to lean on the Creve Coeur committeeman to lean on Johnson. Lew's candidate for judge won the primary but lost the general.

Probably our best political effort was in the defeat of the Democratic "Establishment," led and financed by the Central Missouri Trust Company in the '64 Primary. I helped from the outside because I'd resigned from the committee at the end of '63. Lew had the job of writing our candidate Warren Hearnes's speeches on the environment, then an important issue, unfortunately more so then than now. Lew got most of his material from our old friend Leo Drey, then and still the foremost environmentalist in the state. He also helped me get a small patronage job that aided my up-and-down economy.

At Governor Hearnes's inauguration ceremony in 1965, we were both Missouri colonels. I wore the uniform except for the cap that Lew had bought from a prior colonel, and he wore the uniform I'd rented from another prior, again except for the cap. My head was bigger than Lew's, but his body was larger.

Lew and Louise gave me a ride to Jefferson City and back for Hearnes's second Inaugural Ball in '69. Louise voluntarily sat in the back seat on the way back at night and almost froze, without complaint. I've regretted ever since not changing places with her, for there was enough room for all three of us in the warmer front seat.

In 1965, Lew was appointed first chairman of the new Air Conservation Commission, and during his term he seemed to sour on Hearnes, probably with good reason. He should have thanked Hearnes, though, for being indirectly responsible for his becoming the leading environmental lawyer in the state.

In '65 or '66 Yarmolinsky, then one of McNamara's bright, youngish men called his old friend Lew re the right-wing activities of True Davis, a St. Joe multimillionaire, who wanted to be an assistant secretary of Defense. Lew asked me for help, and I was able to get evidence of such activities from a friend from church who was then a grad student at Lincoln University in Jeff, the only white person there at the time. Davis did not get the appointment.

Lew continued on the committee. In '72 he favored sending an un-committed delegation to the presidential convention. McGovern had many supporters who wanted a pledged delegation. At the Bonhomme mass meeting the McGovern people wanted "winner take all," but Lew was able to beat them, and all the delegates to the Congressional District and State Conventions from Bonhomme were uncommitted.

In '76 Lew was all for Mo Udall for president and prevailed on me to help out. That was probably our last campaign together, and again our candidate did not win. We did not always (often?) support the winner, but we always supported the better one. I'm very glad I knew and worked with Lew, and I miss him.

Anne Green Romig

Romig is one of the Greens' four children, along with Lewis, Jr., Mary, and Kathleen.

It's great to hear about Dad from his friends—behind his legal battles was his wife—he tried out his briefs on Mom and she found him quotes from Shakespeare, or *Alice in Wonderland*, to make his points.

Dad loved dogs, chocolate, and children. He would rather play with the kids than mix with the adults at parties. When we were little, visiting his mother's house, he sat with the kids in another room, rather than stay with the grown-ups at the adult table. We always felt sorry for the grown-ups, because we knew we had more fun, and Dad seemed to think so, too. As both a father and a grandfather, he was always the first to suggest playing games.

Chocolate: Whenever I eat chocolate I think of Dad—and that's pretty much every day. When we were children, growing up in Kirkwood, Dad would walk us down to the Velvet Freeze on hot summer nights for ice cream cones. Velvet Freeze used to have those little placemats for kids to color in with crayons, and every so often, they'd have a competition and hang the placemats in the windows, all over the store. Once Dad wanted to color the placemat, too, so he did, and signed the name of our Cat Lucy, age 4. It was a surprise when Velvet Freeze called and said Lucy had won the competition, and she could come get her free ice cream cone. That night we walked down to Velvet Freeze and after he bought all of our cones, Dad said Lucy was home sick in bed, and could we take her cone to her.

Dogs: And of course Dad loved all dogs, but especially his two Golden Retrievers. Every day at the hospital he asked us to be sure to pet Calvin and Jesse. Even on his busiest work days, when he was focused on deadlines, he would take ten minutes each morning to pet the dogs, even before his morning coffee.

Logic/Latin: Dad believed Latin was critical—it would teach us grammar and logic. In the car as he drove us to school each morning, one of our car games was to recite Latin together: *Hic, haec, hoc, huius, huius, huius;* or *amo, amas, amat.* My husband often blames my inability to understand him on the fact that I'm so literal, so grammatically precise, the way Dad taught us all to be. If someone said, "The plane went down the runway, and it took off," Dad would say, "I don't understand. How could the runway take off?" He wasn't trying to be difficult; he just really didn't understand what you had said, because it wasn't grammatically correct.

Democratic Party: When we were young, Dad was Democratic Committeeman. The Democratic Party seemed to stand for what was just and right and for the interests of the common man. Many of my early memories are about working on Election Day, bringing coffee and doughnuts to the poll workers. It was so exciting. We felt it was so important. And then the election night parties at our house, as poll workers called in the vote counts from each polling place. I think most of the time we didn't win. But that was not the important thing. It felt great to fight the fight, because we believed in what we were doing. Later, Dad felt the Democratic Party had turned away from the people, and he turned away from it. And after he left politics, Dad continued to fight for the public good through his environmental lawsuits.

I was looking forward to celebrating Mom and Dad's fiftieth wedding anniversary next year. Forty-nine years together is a *long* time. And I hope the rest of us can have the love, support, and admiration for our spouses that Mom and Dad have shared.

I'm sure my former Latin teacher Mrs. Rubenstein will correct me later, but here's my best guess: *Pater, te amamus.*

R. ROGER PRYOR

*For more than a decade, Roger Pryor was the face of the Missouri Coalition for the
Environment. He was the Coalition's environmental policy director when it was the
plaintiff in literally dozens of environmental appeals and lawsuits that Green brought on
behalf of clean air, clean water, or free-running streams and rivers. Pryor was an ardent
environmentalist, a trained geologist, and a gifted musician. This was his tribute to Lew
Green, written 15 years before Pryor's untimely death in 1999.*

THE BALLAD OF LEWIS GREEN

TUNE: Rosin the Bow

He challenged Linclay on Earth City;
He said they were on soggy ground.
By the time Lewis had finished rebuttal,
A new developer had to be found.

REFRAIN: A new developer had to be found,
A new developer had to be found,
By the time Lewis finished rebuttal,
A new developer had to be found.

He argued before the Commission
There was no need for Callaway 2.
On this fact, U.E. finally caved in;
It left poor Chuck Dougherty blue.

(REFRAIN SIMILAR TO FIRST VERSE)

The Great River Road is a treasure
Belonging to me and to you.
Lew battled the Corps to a standstill,
Protecting our old river view.

Now, Hancock, he wrote an amendment;
He fooled us in voting it through.
But, bad law is no substitution,
So into this fracas comes Lew.

When resources are taken for granted
By governments—local and state,
Polluters are held in accounting
When Lew moves the courts to "Checkmate!"

I've known him for almost two decades;
And I guess so have many of you.
We're lucky to have such a stalwart—
He's our battling barrister Lew.

This song is sung as a tribute;
I just couldn't say anything mean.
This way, I'm avoiding a lawsuit
From a libelous roast of Lew Green.

A LAWYER'S MIDNIGHT LAMENT

by Louise Green (1999)
(to the tune of The John B. Sails)

'Tis the law that keeps us free
So that's why my clients and me
Through Missouri and federal courts we do roam,
Upholding what's right,
We work late at night.
But my ever-loving wife says I oughta go home.
   Your're working too late
   It's time to come home

   If I didn't have that deadline I could go home.

I've been suing the MSD
Since 1983
To force them to obey the Hancock Law
   You oughta slow down
   Spend more time at home!

   Who'd enforce the Missouri Constitution if I stayed hom?

The Army thinks it great
To bring poison gas to our state
And play at chemical war in Fort Leonard Wood.
But Missouri's got laws,
So we'll make them pause,
And mind our regulations the way they should!
   You oughta slow down
   You're getting too old

   That's not what a working lawyer oughta be told.

The EPA's not enforcing the law!
The Clean Air Act they simply ignore.
So my clients and me are taking them to court.
The polluters are sad,
Senator Bond is mad
To see Missouri citizens take action of this sort.
   You oughta stay home!

   But if I stayed home,
   Who'd make all these government agencies follow the law?

INDEX

About the Authors

Patricia Tummons met Lewis Green when she was writing editorials on environmental issues for the *St. Louis Post-Dispatch* in the 1980s. Since 1990, she has been editor and chief writer for Environment Hawai'i, a monthly publication. She lives in Hilo, Hawai'i.

Florence Shinkle was a feature writer for most of her long career at the *St. Louis Post-Dispatch*. She now lives in Franklin County near the Missouri River Bottoms Lewis Green fought to protect.